A GUY WHO V

The testimony of Richard Oostrum vividly demonstrates the power of God to radically change a person's life. His journey from active homosexual to married father is not simply one of victory. His description of the struggle to allow God to be at the centre of his thoughts and actions is both truthful and engaging and one that every Christian faces no matter what their circumstances. This book is about restoration through dedication to God and therefore holds universal appeal.

Martin Hallet, True Freedom Trust, Wirral, UK

Richard Oostrum's life is a window to love and its power to transform humanity at its core. How Jesus released him from the domination of homosexuality is told with wisdom, compassion and a light touch that lifts it above the usual fare. An important book for those intent on Jesus raising up the age-old foundations in their own lives or in those they love.

Andy Comiskey, Desert Stream Ministries, Anaheim Hill, USA

Once you begin to read this book you won't be able to put it down. It tells the story of how one man's life was changed for ever. Its simple beauty will move you to have hope and faith for yourself and those you love and pray for.

Floyd McClung, All Nations, Kansas City, USA

Richard and his wife Noemia are very special people and I feel privileged to know them, not just as colleagues, but as friends. Richard is a global citizen and an inspiring leader. We have prayed together in Venezuela, visited 'brown cafes' in Amsterdam, cried in Malta, scuba-dived in Egypt. Over the past few years they have been leading the work of YWAM in the Red Light District of Amsterdam and are now launching a new YWAM ministry to those with a similar background of sexual brokenness. Richard has one great desire: pointing others to Jesus Christ. He had good reason to do so. His testimony is proof that God is interested in people, in spite of their brokenness, and that Christ has come to save and restore. This book may cause tears and rejoicing at the same time, but my prayer is that it may be an instrument for radical change in the life of any reader who has not yet experienced the liberating grace of Jesus Christ.

Armando Benner, Director YWAM Amsterdam,
Founder Operacion Timoteo,
Co founder destiNations

A Guy Who Was Gay

The story of Richard Oostrum

HANS FRINSEL

KINGSWAY PUBLICATIONS

EASTBOURNE

ISBN 184291264 X
ISBN 978–1–842912–64–5

01 02 03 04 05 06 Printing/Year 10 09 08 07 06

Published by
KINGSWAY COMMUNICATIONS LTD
Lottbridge Drove, Eastbourne, BN23 6NT, England.
Email: books@kingsway.co.uk

Printed in Canada

Contents

About the Authors

Richard and his wife Noemia have been leading the work of YWAM in the Red Light District of Amsterdam and are now launching a new YWAM ministry to those suffering from sexual brokenness.

Hans Frinsel (1952), former missionary in Guiné-Bissau, is Editor of the Dutch evangelical monthly magazine *De Oogst* (the Harvest) and heads up Oogst Publications, the publishing department of an extensive evangelistic and social work ministry in the Netherlands.

Foreword

The present debate about homosexuality is often heated. I do not want to heat up the discussion further, but simply tell the story of the reality of God in a person's life. His work in the life of Richard Oostrum was both deep and radical, delivering him from the gay lifestyle. This fact in itself may be offensive to some. Even though the tone of the book is not judgemental, God's testimony cannot be ignored.

In order for me to write this book Richard let me look into his life in depth over a period of six months and I greatly admire his openness, sincerity and integrity in the process. It was our goal to be as accurate as possible about his feelings and the facts, but also to be sensitive and fair to the feelings of others. For reasons of privacy some names have been changed, except of those who did not object to being mentioned.

Richard's enthusiasm about the way in which I had captured and worded his experiences gives me confidence that this book paints an honest and true picture of his life. This book is not trying to be sensational. That wouldn't suit Richard's character at all. It does want to be buoyant, dynamic and honest but also urgent. That's who he is.

Richard's motivation in coming out with his story is his deep conviction that he has a precious message of hope to share. God's intervention in his life was both dramatic and real. Jesus Christ filled up a longing that nothing else could satisfy. God healed the sexual brokenness that had enslaved him in addictive behaviour. It is his and my deep desire that others may find hope through these pages.

Hans Frinsel
Amsterdam, 2004

1

Calling

We were standing in formation at the entrance of the imposing Yankee Stadium in New York in nervous anticipation, poised and ready to march forward at the signal and enter the sports arena. This was the big occasion, our event, my moment. The different country delegations marched through the gates, one after the other, in alphabetical order. That meant that we – the Dutch delegation of some 200 athletes – had to wait a while before it was our turn to go forward and take part in the celebration. A big screen outside showed us what was going on inside and made us all the more eager to be part of it. The atmosphere was electric. The adrenalin was rushing through my veins. Impatiently I awaited the signal for us to march and be part of this great happening.

It was the closing ceremony of the Gay Games 1994. This was not just a ceremonial duty to be performed, but to me and many others this was the highlight of these Games. A terrific manifestation of unity and conviction. All of a sudden our delegation started to move and march forward. Now it was our turn. In our red, white and blue training costumes – beautifully designed especially for these Games – we entered the arena. As a deluge, the noise of applause, cheers and acclamation of the 70,000 spectators descended on us. It overwhelmed me completely. I felt totally absorbed in this stadium full of people, all of whom I had something in common with, something very important at the core of my being: my sexual identity. This was a highlight in the struggle of the gay movement, despised, scorned and so often persecuted in the past. For a number of years I myself had wrestled with sexual feelings that did not seem to fit into life as it was supposed to be. I had been fearful of the possible reactions of those who surrounded me, but at my coming out, my family and friends had responded with acceptance and understanding. Yet I had seen so many others who had been treated differently, who had met with condemnation and rejection, had seen family ties severed and had lost friends.

But this was a triumphal march. Now the world could not ignore us. We were a formidable power to be reckoned with. It was an experience of deep solidarity and unity. I moved as in a flush of victory. At this moment we were the centre of attention. All eyes were fixed on us. I was taken up in the event. Here I was one with everybody and every-thing that was happening around me. Now we were at home. Here there was no threat or insecurity. Within the confines of this massive happening we could freely cele-brate our identity and lifestyle. There was nobody to harm us, ridicule us or limit our freedom.

The closing ceremony of the Gay Games is always an occasion marked by an abundance of creativity and expres-sion of all kinds. The gay world is a subculture in which

artistic qualities are plentiful. Here in New York the ceremony had of course a typically American character: huge,
extravagant and glamorous. It was a whirling show, with
performances by such great names as Patti LaBelle and
Cyndi Lauper. As well as musical performances, there were
dancing acts, costumes, parades and of course many inspiring and fiery speeches in which the gay lifestyle was
extolled and confirmed.

I was part of the Dutch swimming team and had com-
peted in the 50-metre butterfly stroke, the 50-metre
freestyle, the 100-metre freestyle and the 100-metre medley. Because of personal circumstances my condition was
not optimal and I had not won any medals in any of the
heats. However, participating was much more important
than carrying away medals. To be there and to feel at one
with the great worldwide gay family was our goal.

Such an event radiates power. Of course we were all
marching to the same music, singing the same tune and listening to the rhetoric that we had heard before, but here
the message was expressed in such impressive and colourful designs and forms that it took full possession of me. This
was the grand finale of the Gay Games in New York, but as
the final accords sent an exhilarating shiver down my spine,
I knew it wasn't over for me. I had found my destiny. I had
a new purpose in life. They had just announced that the
next Gay Games would be held in Amsterdam in 1998, in
my city. I would be there. More than that, I was going to
dedicate the coming years to promoting these Games in the
Netherlands. I felt the passion of an evangelist. It was as if I
had a vision. I could picture the way it should take shape.
Not the same as in New York, of course, but in a way that

suited Amsterdam; on a more modest scale perhaps, as far as size and numbers were concerned, but completely embedded in the culture of our city. Just imagine the locations, with the famous canals in the centre of the city! And which European city was better suited to the gay culture because of its tolerance? Wasn't it often called the gay capital of Europe?

With this goal in mind I travelled back to Holland. More than ever I felt confirmed in my gay identity. I knew who I was, where I belonged and what direction my life would take. My gay identity was now not only a lifestyle. It had become my calling and the gay lifestyle my message.

Four years later, I was indeed at the Gay Games in Amsterdam, but not participating as an athlete in the swimming competition and not even to promote the gay lifestyle. How could my life have taken such a drastic turn? Had I erred in ascertaining my destiny? Had I maybe missed another calling in the past?

2

My Secret

I was born in 1962 and grew up in Voorburg, a suburb of The Hague, the city well known for its 'Peace Palace', the International Court of Justice, and the war tribunal that was set up in the wake of the Bosnian war. Here I spent my childhood, and here I lived and worked for 34 years, close to my family and friends.

I was the second of two children. We formed a very happy family, my parents, my sister Ineke and me. My earliest memories go back to when I was four years old and attending kindergarten. I can still picture my mother, waiting outside the school building to collect my sister and me at midday. The three of us would walk home to have lunch. Home meant so much for me. It was my security, the place of comfort I could run to whenever confronted with the little sufferings you go through as a child: a bruised knee or a squabble with a playmate. Home meant safety. There weren't any serious dangers in our neighbourhood. On the contrary, it was a safe place. But to me there was no place like home. Regularly we would invite school friends to come and join us for lunch and they liked to come because of the relaxed and friendly atmosphere. For some who came from less harmonious backgrounds, our house was a favourite refuge.

We lived in a relatively new lower middle-class suburb, built in the late fifties and so characteristic of post-war Holland, with friendly looking apartment blocks, three or four storeys high, and streets that were made attractive with stretches of grass, shrubs and trees along the pavements. Our small four-room apartment was at ground level, which meant the luxury of a small garden at the back with the usual shed for the bicycles, so typical but also indispensable for life in Holland. The apartment was modestly furnished with the standard furniture of that time, simple but tasteful, with a coal stove in the living room, the very picture of Dutch cosiness in the sixties. Nowadays people scoff at the culture of snugness and good citizenship of those days, but to me it was the secure and warm context in which I could grow up without any anxiety.

All four of my grandparents lived nearby. Family ties were close and they visited us very frequently. As a child I perceived that my mother played a central and dominant role in this harmonious setting. To me she was the king pin. My father was also very much part of that family life, but in my perception his presence and role were much less accentuated. During the day he went to work, of course, but in the evening and at the weekends he was also very often absent. Soccer ruled his life to a great extent and it also determined the agenda of the rest of the family. My father had been a semi-professional soccer player. For years he had been the goalkeeper of ADO, the most popular club in The Hague. When I was two years old, he quit his soccer career, and shortly afterwards he suffered a stroke. For some weeks he was nearly blind and he spent some time in hospital. Surprisingly he recovered completely and as soon as he was fit again, he was asked to train and coach several teams of a local soccer club. Very often he would come home from work, eat quickly and hurry off to the football grounds. During the weekend he had to be there to coach the team and generally we would accompany him, spending much of the day at the football club.

Although in the early sixties professional soccer in Holland had not yet developed into the billion dollar business it is now, it was the favourite national sport in Holland. Because of his history as a professional player, my father enjoyed a certain amount of popularity, certainly in our part of the country, even after he stopped playing himself. My mum felt as much at home in the world of soccer as my dad did. They had first met at the soccer club and this sport was a staple ingredient of the daily conversation in our home.

'And Richard, do you like to play soccer? Do you want to become a professional player when you grow up? Do you want to be as good as your dad was?' These were the questions I was so often asked as a child. And they made me feel distinctly awkward, because soccer did not interest me at all. But in most cases I did not have to reply to these questions. My father would do that for me, referring to an incident that happened when I was three or four years old. We had gone for a walk through the dunes along the coast and my father had brought along a football, meaning to play with me and teach me to kick the ball around. But however hard he tried, he couldn't interest me in the ball. My

attention was constantly diverted to the beautiful surroundings and the vegetation of the dune landscape.
Instead of kicking the ball back to him, I started to pick
flowers. My dad would tell this story as a solid proof that I
most likely would not follow in his footsteps.

Soccer being sport number one in Holland, every Dutch
father will have been out at times, kicking a ball about with
his children. And quite naturally many a father feels a
touch of pride when his four-year-old son returns a pass
correctly or scores a goal. As a prejudiced parent he immediately pictures him as a new star in the international soccer
arena. My father always told the anecdote in good humour.
He wholeheartedly accepted the fact that his son would not
follow a soccer career and he never tried to force me to
develop a love for this sport. I was as much his son without
any interest for his favourite sport. Yet I heard the story of
the failed attempt to get me to play soccer so often that I
unconsciously interpreted it as a suppressed disappointment. I felt I could not fully live up to the expectations of
my environment.

Family life was very important to me. Doing things
together gave me a strong feeling of belonging. Those
moments were highlights in my childhood. I can vividly
remember witnessing the arrival of the first men on the
moon. It was very early in the morning and my mother had
woken my sister and me up to see this great event. We were
all sitting on my parents' bed, intently watching the old
black and white TV set, and I can still recall every ingredient of the breakfast we ate on that occasion.

Because of his work and his busy soccer programme, the
moments my father could dedicate exclusively to me were

scarce. Probably because they were so few, these moments are indelibly imprinted on my memory. From the time I was eight years old, we spent our summer holiday camping in Austria or Italy. Those were highlights, as my father spent most of this time with my sister and me. I played for hours with him, imagining adventures, following the course of a brook, building dams to divert its course, collecting beautiful stones that sparkled as gold under the water but unfortunately lost most of that beauty when dried up. My father would enter into my games. When I was old enough, he took me out canoeing on the lake, and I thoroughly enjoyed each precious moment of being alone with him.

I went to primary school and learning came easyily to me. My grades were above average. From the start I was often attracted to the weaker children in the class, the 'losers'. I felt a solidarity with them and an urge to take their side. There was one girl in particular who seemed to be a natural outsider. She was often bullied and I tried to protect her, but I also made an effort to involve her and build bridges to the rest of the group.

I could get on well with everybody and I never lacked playmates. Many children wanted to be my friend, but strangely enough I did not have a special friend. As a child I never developed that close and intimate type of friendship in which you can share your deeper feelings; a friendship to last, with a friend I could really confide in.

In the early seventies a new phenomenon was introduced in our suburb: the bottle bank. Containers were placed at different locations in the neighbourhood, where people were asked to put their non-returnable glass bottles. This was a very interesting development for us as children, because we soon found out that along with the non-returnable bottles, people would by accident or out of sheer laziness also throw away bottles on which there was still a deposit. When the container was full enough, we would rummage through the bottles we could reach and sort out the ones for which we could get the deposit back. This made for an easy and welcome addition to our pocket-money. The square gin bottles in particular were prized game, as they had a high deposit.

One morning, as I was going to school, I passed the bottle bank and decided to do a quick inspection. When feeling around for bottles, I came across some paper instead. Curious, I drew it out. It was a pornographic magazine. It was so revolting and extreme that it shocked me deeply. I was absolutely bewildered. At nine years of age I was quite innocent and had not as yet had any sex education. I was completely unprepared for the pictures that confronted me and they filled me with deep disgust and a feeling of nausea. At that age you accept the differences between men and women as a matter of fact. They had never given rise to any questions in my mind. They were not spelled out emphatically in my environment. My parents were not particularly secretive about these matters, but decency marked our lifestyle and open nudity certainly had no place in our home. This pornographic magazine was my first confrontation with the uncovered female body. Yet it showed much more than that and what I saw was so dirty and incomprehensible to me that it made me feel sick.

This was an extreme and premature confrontation with sexuality and it forced a distorted image of sex on my mind. Yet although I found it revolting, at the same time it caused a strange feeling of excitement. It repelled me, but also made me curious. It was as though I had been given a sneaky view of some secret and forbidden world. Although it made me scared, I took the magazine with me to school to share this extreme experience with my friends. Right afterwards I threw the magazine out and felt relieved.

The sordid images kept milling through my head for quite some time. This was my first impression of sexuality and it was destructive. As a child you are vulnerable and first impressions are so important. This information was damaging to me and caused me to develop a distorted idea of sexuality. Several years later during my adolescence, when sexual feelings began to play a role, the images of the women in the pornographic magazine would often pop up in my mind.

Another new and strong influence that I experienced at school was of a completely different nature. It also had a long-lasting effect on my life. The school I went to was a state school. In contrast to the many Catholic and Protestant schools, the state schools did not include any religious elements in their general curriculum. However, as there were always parents who wanted some form of religious instruction for their children, our school offered the possibility of an hour of religious teaching each week for a couple of years. This service even went so far as to provide a choice between instruction by a Protestant pastor or instruction by a Catholic priest. God and religion were matters that lay completely outside my experience and did not play any role in our family. My parents and grandparents had had unfavourable experiences with the church as an institution. Things had happened in the past that had made them antagonistic to anything related to the church, and as a matter of fact they had chosen to send my sister and me to a state school.

However, for some reason or other, I fancied going to the religious instruction class, though it was optional. I had heard that the pastor who usually took those classes could tell beautiful Bible stories. I had absolutely no idea what Bible stories were, but I knew I did like to hear stories. I asked my parents for permission. They told me what they thought about the church, but they were of the opinion that a little bit of knowledge about religion could do me no harm. 'We cannot teach you anything about religion ourselves, as we do not know much about it, but it is good that you do know something about it as a part of your education.'

So, off to the religious instruction class I went. At first I really felt out of place. Pastor Steenhuizen, who taught the class, tried to find out what we knew of the Bible. He asked many questions and, in contrast to most of the others, I didn't know a single answer. He must have wondered at my being there at all. It made me feel uncomfortable. The pastor was sensitive to my position, however, and tried to involve me in different ways in order to make me feel at home. He would ask me questions that did not require a lot of previous knowledge, such as those involving arithmetic, which was my favourite subject. 'The Old Testament contains 39 books and the New Testament 27. What is the total number of books in the Bible?' This helped to make me feel at home, but I did not need much persuasion to continue to attend his classes, as he had a way of telling Bible stories that really captured my full attention. Here was another unknown and mysterious world to which I was introduced, yet this time it was not shocking or revolting. It attracted me. Strangely enough, in later years, I noticed that I could not remember much about the Bible stories that fascinated me back then. The story of Moses and the pictures he showed us were the only things I could recall in some detail.

There was something else about Pastor Steenhuizen's lessons that always stuck with me. As we sat in a circle and he finished his story, he would say, 'And now we will pray.' Then all heads were bowed, eyes closed and hands folded together and he would say a prayer. This was all strange to me. The first time I heard him pray it made a deep impression on me – talking to someone you couldn't see, but who was there; talking to the God who made everything. It was an awesome thought, but at the same time it gave me a sense of safety and peace.

'You can do the same at home,' the pastor encouraged us. 'For instance, you can pray before you go to sleep. That's a good moment to talk to God. You can pray for your father and mother, or for a friend who is sick. You can tell God about the things that happened during the day. You can also tell him of the things that you have done wrong and ask him to forgive you. You can ask him to help you in the things that you find difficult or of which you are afraid. And then you can end your prayer in the same way we do here: in Jesus' name, amen.'

Talking to God! I decided there and then that I would take up his advice. I think that deep inside me there was a strong desire to do this. I needed someone to talk to, someone with whom I could share my feelings, my deeper emotions and thoughts. So I started to say my prayers every evening before going to sleep, kneeling at my bedside. It was a simple prayer with a very fixed pattern. I remember I always used to insert the phrase 'forgive me if I have taken your name in vain'. This was something I had picked up during the religious instruction class, but I didn't have the foggiest notion what it meant. It sounded serious enough, though, to be included in the prayer. I prayed for my parents, my sister and my grandparents, but also about problems I experienced and things that bothered me.

I did not tell my parents about my prayers. Instinctively I felt that they wouldn't approve of too much religion and that prayer might be something they hadn't reckoned with when giving me permission to attend the religious instruction classes. This might be just a little bit too much for them. Before praying, I would check there was nobody near my room. I said my prayer audibly – that was the way I had learned to pray in school and I did not know another way of doing it – yet I would drop my voice to a tiny whisper, to be sure that anybody outside my bedroom door could not hear anything. What I was saying only concerned God. I did not want anybody to know. This was my secret, or rather a secret between God and me. It turned into a life-long habit.

As a child it is difficult to discern whether things you come into contact with are good or bad, especially when it concerns spiritual matters. I had an inquisitive nature and was always ready to try new things. In the fifth grade we had a teacher who came from the Surinam in South America. He had evidently dabbled in occult practices and regularly introduced elements of these in the class. He attempted to teach us to read one another's minds. It turned out I could make telepathic contact with a girl in the class. It was fascinating and scary at the same time. Another trick he involved us in was even more spectacular. He sat on a chair and asked four of us to stand around him. I made sure I was one of the four, always being game for experiments. We had to lay our hands on his head and push down as hard as possible. Then at his signal, we each had to put our own index fingers together, tips pointing, and each child had to place their two fingers either under one of his armpits or under his knees. Then we had to lift him. And we did! Even though it took some effort on our part, I do not think that under normal circumstances four ten-year-olds can lift a fair-sized adult just using their index fingers. It was eerie. Here were unseen powers at work. I did not connect this in any way to what I learned in the religious classes, but all things spiritual fascinated me.

With this mixed bag of spiritual luggage I moved on to secondary education.

3

The Deep End

I might not have been destined for a soccer career, but this did not mean I did not like sports. I particularly liked swimming. The Netherlands is well known for its rivers and innumerable canals. For safety reasons children there are taught to swim at an early age. I passed my first swimming test at the age of six and it was soon obvious that I had talent in this sport.

One day when swimming in a local swimming pool I was noticed and singled out by an official of a swimming club, who was scouting around for young talent. He approached me and my parents to ask whether I would like to join the training of the competition section of their club for a try out. I was eight years old at the time, but as keen as mustard. My parents agreed readily. They were eager to see me doing something in a sports competition that meant regular and disciplined training.

I enrolled as a member of the swimming club and soon I was involved in serious training and preparation for the swimming competition. I got up at 5:30 every morning, quickly had a bite to eat and then jumped on my bicycle to peddle to the swimming pool. We trained from six to seven in the morning. This required endurance on my part, but also sacrifice on the part of my parents. I was still very young and at first my mother did not let me cycle alone to the swimming pool so early in the morning. She would come along, wait till I had finished my training and then take me home again. Back home we had a quick breakfast and then I would hurry off to school. It was a hectic life, but I thoroughly enjoyed it. An additional encouragement was that my sister also joined the swimming club and attended the same training sessions. Now we could go together.

'Mum, you don't have to come along any more. We are old enough to go to the swimming pool on our own,' we urged. It would save her a lot of bother and time, but she wasn't easily persuaded. She was always a little over-anxious and very reluctant to relinquish control and let her children fend for themselves. In the end she gave in, but the first few times we went alone she just waited for us to disappear around the corner, then quickly put on her coat, jumped on her bike and rode to the swimming pool by an alternative route. There she would wait and watch just to make sure we arrived safely. We never noticed.

My sister Ineke and I did many things together during our childhood and this forged a close bond between us. We were always together. We shared many interests and though she was more than a year older, we even shared the same friends, or rather I played with Ineke's friends more than I did with my schoolmates.

'Why don't you bring along one or two of your friends from school? I would love to meet some of your school-mates,' my mum would urge me regularly. She would like to see me play with my natural peers. And dutifully I did. The next day I took John home and presented him at the front door. 'Mum, this is John.'

'Hello, John. Nice to see you.'

'Mum, can we have some sweets?'

'Of course.'

I left John standing at the front door, went in to get the sweets, gave John some, then said goodbye and closed the door on him.

'Why did you do that?' my mother exclaimed.

'You wanted me to bring a school friend home, didn't you? Well, I did!' I had done what was asked of me, but I had no intention of playing with him.

By the time my sister went on to secondary education, she began to attend the swimming training sessions less frequently and I often went there alone. Her interests changed and so did her activities. She entered early into her adolescence and because of that our age difference became more significant. But though we did not share in many activities any more and we both had our separate lives, a strong tie remained between us.

Swimming had become my passion and I made good progress. I wanted to perform as best I could, especially when medals and prizes were at stake. It made me really proud when on Monday morning in school I could show the medals I had won at the weekend.

Sometimes we received critical remarks from neighbours or relatives: 'Isn't it too demanding for such a young boy to get up so early in the morning every day of the week, to follow such a heavy training programme?' Indeed, I spent an average of ten hours a week in the swimming pool, but to me it wasn't difficult. I loved every minute of it. Of course there were moments when I was less enthusiastic and mornings when I'd rather roll over in bed once more than get up at the crack of dawn to rush off to a heavy training session. But I always quickly got over those moments of reluctance, packed my bag and went off. I had a strong desire to improve my performance and I knew that this required self-discipline and sacrifice. Swimming had become my life. My times were good and by the age of ten I was fully involved in the competition. It was all so exciting and thrilling. I always looked forward to the matches with eager anticipation.

Entering the swimming arena, the warm damp atmosphere and the smell of chlorine seemed to embrace me and make me part of the whole. I would receive my participation card and feel the adrenaline level rise. I had been working towards this moment during training and now had to prove myself. There were generally some 50 or 60 of us, all children of the same age group, standing together, impatiently looking around, shifting from one leg to the other. One after another would disappear for a quick visit to the toilet to ease the suspense. Then my name or number was called and I came forward and handed in my card. Now I was on my own as I stepped on the block for the next heat. And I had just one goal: to set the best time and be the fastest.

At that time I had one more ambition: I needed to swim within certain time limits in order to qualify for the national competition. And I managed to achieve this. In the Dutch competition I excelled at the butterfly stroke, the crawl and the backstroke. Breaststroke was not my strongest discipline.

Whenever I smell chlorine or the air of a swimming pool, it instantly conjures up all those memories and sometimes even literally causes the same feeling of tension in my stomach, the healthy nervousness that would take hold of me. Then I can recall vividly the atmosphere of the swimming pool in The Hague, where I swam most of the qualification matches. Taking part in the national competition also meant that as a child I travelled to a lot of other towns and cities in the country. Each time it meant new surroundings, new faces and making new acquaintances, but always with the swimming arena as the central focus of all of these activities.

When I was twelve years old, I began participating in international competitions and had to make trips to other countries. At that age such events were exhilarating experiences. Germany and Belgium share a common border with Holland so were quite near, but going to Britain meant crossing the sea. This was a big adventure. I was staying with a local family and for the first time in my life I had to try to make myself understood by using the little English I had learned in school. All of a sudden life was not only exciting, but also serious. My horizon began to expand.

Around the same time, while I was still very much involved in the competition, the water polo section of the swimming club asked me whether I would join them too. I loved to watch water polo, which in those days was a very popular sport in the Netherlands. Our country had at that time the largest water polo competition in the world and our national team had just won the bronze medal at the Olympic Games. As a country we had a great name in this sport, especially our ladies' team. The idea of playing some water polo besides competition swimming appealed to me.

There was always an element of competition between the water polo section of the club and the swimming competition section in trying to enlist good swimmers. You always had to choose one or the other. Doing both was not really regarded as an option and understandably so. The swimming technique in both sports is very different. In water polo you swim with your head above water. The lower part of the body automatically drops lower down into the water and you make short strokes to guide the ball before you. In a swimming contest you must go through the water horizontally and make long strokes. If you combine this form of swimming with water polo, your technique goes by the board, you 'lose your stroke', as they say, and your times will suffer. That was not in the interest of the club or the competition.

I had the tendency to be a bit of a 'loner' in the swimming club. Not that I wanted to be a loner. I just was. I always got on well with the other children, but though I had many contacts, for some reason I did not have really close friendships. Swimming is an individual sport and this in a sense enhanced my tendency to be alone. The moment you get on the starting block, you're all on your own. I had gone for it with the right kind of mentality: I wanted to win and be the best.

But now I noticed that what attracted me to water polo was the aspect of team sport and I decided to accept the invitation. I enjoyed working together with others towards a common goal. This was an element I had missed out on before. My mindset did not change. I was still as ambitious as before and gave myself fully. I still wanted to win and perform well and I was determined to contribute something worthwhile to the team. And I succeeded. Often I was top scorer of the team. At home they heartily supported this development. Water polo as a team sport and ball sport was much more akin to soccer and was therefore much more to the taste of my soccer-loving family.

To the surprise of my team mates and the club I managed to combine water polo and competition swimming quite well and continued in both. In this way I enjoyed the satisfaction of individual performance as well as team spirit. I never regretted this choice. I soon noticed that team spirit continues even after the last whistle of the match. The water polo team developed into a solid group of friends. We went out together, organised parties and other activities. This resulted in friendships that lasted for many years.

Swimming and water polo are macho sports, requiring strength. You cannot play water polo and be squeamish. I felt at home in those sports and earned the respect of my team mates because of my performance. There was only one snag, one uncomfortable bump in my otherwise smooth and perfect sports life: I had been given a nickname. In itself this wasn't a strange thing, as many of my friends in the swimming club were called by nicknames. The unpleasantness was in the particular nickname they had stumbled on: 'Fatty'. To be honest, I couldn't blame them, because as a child I was positively chubby. It never bothered me, and it certainly did not hamper my swimming performance, as was borne out by the good results. Perhaps people hadn't expected me to do so well and were surprised. Being fat and engaging in top sport are mutually exclusive at first sight. The image the general public has of

a sportsman is someone with a slender figure, or alter-
natively with impressive muscles, but certainly without any
fat at all! The nickname was used in good humour, however
– never with the intention of bullying me or putting me
down. I was a fully accepted member of the club. Perhaps
the nickname rather expressed admiration at the fact that
somebody with my build could perform so well. All the
same, deep inside me I did not appreciate that name. It worried me. It made me feel different. Was I different from the
rest?

In the end, I never had to do anything to lose weight,
because approaching the age of 14, all of a sudden I began
to grow tall and lost every ounce of fat. In fact if anyone
were to call me by my old nickname now, people would
certainly think it was meant ironically, perhaps to induce
me to eat more, as I am positively skinny.

4

Teenage Dream

My childhood had been carefree. I enjoyed the security of a happy home and a sport that gave me a sense of achievement. At primary school, learning had come easily to me and paying attention during classes had been enough to secure good results. Homework was something I hardly knew. All hours not spent in school or at the swimming pool, I had used to play outside with my sister and my friends.

When I left primary school I was advised to enter secondary school at the higher level. In Holland secondary education can be entered at two or three different levels, according to the pupil's ability. As a child I looked forward to this new period in my life. It felt like entering the adult world. This was for real!

Yet the first class of secondary school hit me like a freight train. I had expected to be able to continue my carefree existence, only to find out that 'real life' was really serious. Homework turned out not to be just an abstract word; it had to be taken seriously. This required a totally different mindset on my part, for which I had not been prepared.

Things that came easily to me before all of a sudden required a fair amount of exertion, time and perseverance. These qualities I knew well enough, but only in relation to swimming. Schoolwork had always taken second place and had never been a priority with me.

In common with most other teenagers, I found that the serious study requirements of secondary school came at an inconvenient time. At that age there are so many new things to be discovered. I made new friends and our class organised parties. The adolescent phase announced itself. Conversations shifted from kids' stuff to talking about girls. Sexuality began to play an increasing role. Girls became a fascinating subject for us as boys, and the other way around.

With a number of classmates, both boys and girls, we soon formed a group of friends. We regularly met outside school hours. Every Friday afternoon we would meet at Stefan's. His parents lived in a beautiful old villa in one of the posh neighbourhoods of our town. It had a large attic, part of which Stefan's parents had allowed him to use as a 'teenage den' with his friends. He had filled it with some old furniture and fixed it up in the style of our youth culture. It was the time of 'flower power', the hippie movement, and we admired that culture. We played our records and talked about the popular subjects of our generation: freedom, kicking against the establishment, the sexual revolution. It all sounded very important, but it didn't really rise above the level of irresponsible teenage talk.

Love and dating were of course part and parcel of the life within this group, but for all the talk about free love, in practice we hardly went beyond kissing, though there were the first careful experiments with the phenomenon of sexuality. I joined in, not because of any desire, but rather because I wanted to conform to the group. In fact in those early days I had but a vague idea what sexuality really entailed.

At home I talked about all the new things I experienced at school. Washing-up was a chore my sister and I did together with my mother and it became the time for talking about the day's events, and also discussing serious matters. My mother was the centre of the family and if we had anything serious to discuss, we would take it to my mother first. Later, only if necessary, we would talk about it with my dad.

My mother kept a careful watch over what we did, always being a bit over-anxious. As a teenager I had few secrets from my mother, but instinctively I felt I should not dwell on the details of what we did in Stefan's attic. One evening, when chatting to my mother while drying the dishes, she broached the subject herself: 'Tell me, Richard, what do you and your friends do exactly up in that attic at Stefan's on Friday afternoon?'

I was alarmed and wondered why she had asked. How much did she know? I stumbled over my words as I tried to give her an answer in the form of a half-truth. It did not fool her. She evidently knew more.

'Yesterday evening I met Stefan's mother at the information meeting in school and she told me some things that I feel concerned about. She thinks it's wonderful to have you all meeting in the attic, listening to music and all that. I don't mind that. But she also thinks it rather cute that you folks try to discover for yourselves what sex is all about. She has some modern ideas about that. She may approve, but I feel concerned. I think you should be very careful what you do.'

Knowing my mother, I could imagine how she reacted when Stefan's mother glowingly told her about the goings on in the attic. She probably kept her mouth tightly shut and went home very worried. Although sexuality wasn't a great taboo in our home, my parents believed in decency and above all in responsible conduct in this area.

My grades at the end of the first year in secondary school were only just good enough to get me into the second year. I had managed to get through that year with only minimum attention to my homework and that had suited me well. But this is of course not the attitude that will take you through secondary school, and the second year became a crisis year as far as my studies were concerned. I failed and had to do that year again. My parents weren't over-ambitious with regard to the education of their children, but they knew I could do better than that and were very concerned with my lack of progress. Visits to the school and talks with the principal followed. My parents had never punished us severely. That hadn't been necessary. I couldn't stand it when my parents were angry with me. Just a good telling off generally sufficed to make me toe the line. They quite rightly didn't try to find fault with the school for my bad results, but they did not know how to get me in line this time.

When I finished the second year for the second time, my grades were just good enough to let me pass. The prospect wasn't bright. The school I went to was rather a posh school with pupils from rich homes, though I was of normal middle-class stock. The school had a special fund to send one or two students from each year to a special school when for some reason or other they did not do well in their studies but in fact had enough talent to do better. My parents decided to try and apply for help from this fund, as they couldn't afford such an extra expense themselves. But the principal did not even want to consider our request. Instead he advised me to go to another secondary school with a lower level. Yet the son of the principal was given a grant from the same fund to go to this special school, as he was also not doing well in his studies. My mother was furious. Modest as she was in most circumstances, now she marched to the school to demand an explanation. She didn't succeed in getting a satisfactory answer, but she radiated solidarity when she came out of the office. This time my mother didn't take sides with the school. She took my side and enrolled me in another school. She believed in me and was sure that with their support I would make it.

There was one other matter that worried me at that time, but I did not dare to share it with anybody, not even my parents. I had a strange dream one night. I dreamt about a boy in my class I would go around with occasionally. It was a sexual dream. This boy wasn't anybody special – he was plain and certainly not the hero of the class. The dream frightened me and yet in some way it also felt good. This perturbed me and made me feel insecure. Was I attracted to boys? At first this notion was still hazy to me, but when I was over 14 it began to take clearer shape. Then I noticed that this dream had not been an isolated incident. It turned into a definite interest in boys. I began to see a pattern. Slowly it dawned on me that this was developing in the direction of homosexuality.

My understanding of homosexuality was vague and fragmented. My knowledge on this subject consisted mainly of the usual macho talk and nicknames such as pansy and sissy boy. And then there were all the coarse jokes they used to tell about gays, which made you feel that you definitely did not want to be one of them. This was all the more reason not to talk about my feelings and uncertainties. I sensed that saying anything about this would only incur trouble. This was a secret I guarded really well.

As those feelings frightened me, I began to develop an internal 'early warning' system. I became more cautious in choosing my words and thought carefully about how to move and behave. I became very alert to not saying or doing anything that might betray something about my sexual feelings. Whenever conversation tended in that direction, immediately an internal alarm bell went off. I was always on guard. Generally I did not participate in conversations about sex and girls, but when I did it was only to camouflage my real feelings. This of course meant that I was going around with a constant tension inside. I kept functioning normally in school and within my group of friends at the swimming club, but I constructed a careful division between my internal and my external life. That resulted in loneliness, though I spent a lot of time with others. It was impossible to talk to anyone about those confusing inclinations. The only place where I felt I could safely express my deepest worries was in the quiet of my bedroom, when I said my prayers, which I faithfully kept doing each night. Here I could pour out my heart to God and verbalise my questions. He could help me, couldn't he? I told him urgently that I did not want these feelings. They did not

belong to life as I knew it in our family, in our neighbourhood, at school and in my circle of friends. I did not want to
be different and I certainly did not want to be queer. Yet
these feelings kept bothering me. They became a torture. In
desperation I begged God to take them away and often I
cried bitter tears when praying. Why didn't he do something to change me?

My inner alarm system was very sensitive and it began to
distort reality. It caused me to apply the words and remarks
of others to myself and my sexual feelings. Generally these
remarks had nothing to do with me or with homosexuality,
but because of my fear of being found out, I interpreted
every dubious word as a confirmation of my being different.

I was 16 years old when one of my mates in the water
polo team made a remark that cut me deeply. He was a
macho-type of guy and a joker, always blurting out anything that came into his mind. We were taking a shower
after the match when he jokingly cried out: 'Hey, Richard,
you've got women's legs.' Such ribald remarks were often
made when we were in the showers or getting dressed.
They were uttered in jest. He could have said the same thing
to any member of the team – it was just a bit of good-
natured leg-pulling. Yet because of my inner insecurity, I
took it very personally and it went very deep. *Isn't homosexuality always linked to femininity? There must be something
feminine about me!* I thought. This incident was an un-
welcome confirmation to me, which seemed to insinuate:
'Can't you see? The others have noticed something. It is
obvious to them that you are different!' As an adolescent I
only heard a few remarks like this one, but they struck me
hard. I absorbed them and they took root inside. Slowly

they changed my self-image. My uncertainty increased, and little by little I developed an inferiority complex. The tensions grew and at times resulted in hyperventilation.

To the outside world I was part of the group, but there were many things that made me feel different and out of place. I was always very conscious of the things I couldn't participate in. The interest of the average 16-year-old Dutch boy invariably turns to mopeds, which you are allowed to ride at that age. Anything motorised and speedy is considered macho. Yet I did not have a technical bent and mopeds or cars didn't interest me in the least. Then there was all the macho talk about girls and conquests, which I couldn't enter into either. I avoided such conversations as much as possible. But aren't these the very things that are often regarded as basic to the image of 'healthy' masculinity? At least it became the standard by which I measured myself. I regarded myself less macho, less of a man than the other boys. Yet in reality there wasn't any reason to do so! On the contrary, water polo is a macho sport. You need to be tough to play this game, and I was good at it and didn't hesitate to lead the team.

Naturally I was very careful in the way I approached other boys. I avoided showing my feelings at all costs. Strangely enough I had no idea what consequences my sexual feelings would have for the future. Thinking about the future I did not take my homosexual feelings into consideration at all. Somewhere in the back of my mind I had a hazy notion that one day I would get married and have a family. That was the normal course of events: you get to know a girl, you fall in love, and you get married, build a career and have children. That was reality as I had always experienced it. I had grown up in a harmonious family, which served as a positive example of this life, and I rather expected that this would happen to me one day. Not now, but later. . . much later, as something that happens as a matter of course. I accepted that as the fixed reality of life. Those other feelings would dissolve one day, wouldn't they?

In this light it wasn't strange that during that same period I believed myself to be in love with one of the girls in my class and she was my girlfriend for a while. I really liked to be with her and I noticed that kissing and touching her was not at all unpleasant, yet I also had to admit that somehow it felt incongruous to me. For the time being I accepted that I had to learn to live with that fact.

At that stage of my life the possibility of ever having a relationship with a boy never even entered my head. It was difficult for me to see any positive side to these homosexual feelings. Up till now they had only caused me internal misery. Those deviant feelings made me different and that bothered me. I loathed them. I didn't even want to name them for what they were. I avoided thinking about the future and lived exclusively for the present. The future was too complex. And all the while I masked my inner confusion and fears carefully by an exuberant and superficial exterior. Sport and parties were all my life.

I finished secondary school. It had been easy for me, academically, because I had studied at a level that was below my abilities. I decided that I wanted to continue my studies and go to teacher training college. For some time it had been my wish to become a teacher, as I liked giving instruction. The swimming club had asked me to train and instruct younger groups, and apart from enjoying this greatly it turned out that I had a natural gift for such a job.

However, in the late seventies there was a very high unemployment rate in the educational sector in Holland and the school advised me to enrol for a course in commerce and accountancy, which held brighter prospects of finding a job afterwards. Following on from that I would still have the option of doing a teacher training course in a shorter time and work as a teacher in that field.

I acted on this advice and enrolled in a college that was situated on the other side of The Hague. It was a long way by bike, the normal Dutch means of transport for students, but I enjoyed the early morning ride straight through that beautiful town with its diverse neighbourhoods and residential areas. I also enjoyed the new college and the new people I met there. As I was always careful to keep my deepest feelings hidden from the outside world, it was refreshing to enter a completely new environment, where nobody knew me. It gave me the assurance that certainly nobody could have any inkling as to my inner secret.

As usual I quickly found a new circle of friends and I went around with them throughout my time at college. We went to pubs together and regularly organised parties. We even went on holiday together a few times, to Spain in the summer and a skiing holiday in Switzerland in the winter. I participated fully, but cautiously avoided giving the slightest indication of my true feelings. At certain moments I kept my distance. When the boys started their macho talk about their sexual prowess, I didn't feel comfortable. 'I'll go for a little stroll around the block' was my usual reaction. Sometimes I wondered whether this reaction gave me away. At the time I thought not, but looking back I would say that they probably thought I was so decent and correct on the issue of sexuality it made them wonder.

Within this circle of college friends there was a girl I got on with very well. She was rather a dominant type, too dominant for my mother's liking. We had lots of fun together in college. We danced together at parties and also kissed. She was my girlfriend for quite a while and I noticed that my feelings went beyond a mere infatuation. I really felt attracted to her – she was a beauty. When other boys in our class paid attention to her, it made me feel jealous. Evidently I loved her in some way and she was more to me than just a casual girlfriend. Yet at the back of my mind there were doubts all the time. My attraction to her wasn't sexual. I greatly appreciated her warm friendship, but to me that was as far as it went. I did not want to get enmeshed in a relationship that involved sex. That was a no-go area for me. What I failed to notice was that she had very different expectations on that score. To her just friendship and some kissing was probably not what she wanted to settle for. I had taken it for granted that her expectations were similar to mine. That was a rather naïve supposition and the result of course was that after some time we broke up. For friendships she had her girlfriends; from me she expected something more.

Due to the years of isolation caused by my inner life and because of my internal alarm system, I had developed my own ideas about the world around me, which deprived me of a realistic idea of how others regarded me. I didn't realise that to others I was just the usual heterosexual boy. In fact it never took much effort on my part to attract the attention of a girl. I had noticed that I could make use of that, or even abuse it, but I didn't fully appreciate the expectations this would raise with the girl. Such expectations I had in the meantime already more or less excluded for myself. In my prayers at night I had so often begged God to take the homosexual inclinations away, yet he hadn't done so. What did this mean? Evidently I had to accept this fact. It was certainly not my choice – quite the contrary in fact – but it seemed I had to live with it. To me the reality of these feelings was clear. To my environment they were hidden. I had no idea how to integrate these feelings practically into my life. I did not even want to think of the implications. I postponed any thought about that to the future. But this meant that the Richard inside did not correspond with the Richard outside and those two were driven further apart each day. I was increasingly living a double life. The tension grew and in the end became unbearable.

5

Double Life

By the time I had finished the college course my career ambitions had changed considerably. Instead of going on to teacher training college or to an office job, I had decided to enrol for nurse's training. During the summer holidays I had worked in a nursing home for old people. My job was just to do the cleaning, but I was often called by patients who needed help. I felt a deep concern for these people, a sentiment that was probably strengthened by the fact that my grandparents, with whom I had a close relationship, were suffering ill-health.

However, once again my plans were thwarted, yet this time not by contrary advice, but by the Ministry of Defence. In those days Holland still had a conscription army, and at the age of 18 all boys were called up, although in general only a limited number were actually drafted in. At first it seemed I would escape this nuisance, as we had been informed that the '62 draft was not going to be called up at all. There were constant cut-backs in the size of the army. Then I received the unpleasant news that the Ministry had decided to exempt only the first half of the '62 draft. They apparently considered the second half as absolutely indispensable to the defence of the realm. Unfortunately I had been born on the 8th July, a week too late, and was duly called up. I applied for postponement in order to do nurse's training first, but my request was turned down, as I had already completed one college course. I was very disappointed, not only because of my study plans, but also because like many in my generation I regarded myself as a pacifist. I was not really active in the anti-war movement, but I had joined in the demonstrations against the proliferation of nuclear arms.

Apart from upsetting my career, military service also threatened my sports activities. Our water polo team played in the national competition and the club also counted on me as a trainer of the younger teams.

I wondered how I could wriggle out of national service. I considered becoming a conscientious objector, but the chairman of the swimming club suggested a better idea. He held a high post at the Ministry of Defence and told me he could pull a few strings: 'As a conscientious objector you only make the situation worse, because you will have to do a longer alternative service and you never know where. I can make sure you will get an administrative job here in The Hague. That means you will have to do only six months of field training elsewhere and then you'll be back here working at the Ministry. Look at it as a badly paid job to fill a year of military service, but it will allow you to continue playing water polo and train the other teams. This way you'll miss only six months.'

That sounded like a good alternative. Strangely enough I had to wait more than a year before I actually entered military life. Evidently the urgency to get the '62 draft up to battle standard was not so great after all. Yet in keeping with the impenetrable logic of the army, postponement for the sake of study remained an impossibility. I spent that year doing odd jobs through an agency.

Leaving college also meant losing friends. More than before I now dedicated my time to water polo and my mates in the team. Soon we spent every weekend together. We went into town and to discos, but we also met at one another's homes, where we would sit talking, joking and boozing deep into the night. Whether training for and playing a match or hanging out at a bar with them, I managed to keep up a macho appearance, acting like them, talking like them. But deep inside, in my own identity and in my private life, things were going wrong. My feelings of inferiority were growing alarmingly. When looking at others I only noticed the things I seemed to lack. I didn't see my own strong points. I was easy to approach and a lot of people would come to me for a heart-to-heart talk whenever something was troubling them, yet I did not value these caring qualities in myself. The internal tension mounted.

It was during the year prior to going into the army that I fell in love with a boy for the first time. He was one of my water polo friends, which made the situation rather uncomfortable and complex. The feelings were so strong that in the end I decided to tell him. It was a huge and difficult step to take, but I did not know what else to do. He made it very clear that these feelings were not mutual. Of course I should have expected this, but still his reply cut me up. As this all happened within our close-knit group of friends, I decided to come out into the open. We went around together so much and so intensely that a thing like this could never remain hidden for very long. I considered it would be better to tell them myself rather than let all kinds of gossip or speculation become rampant. My 'coming out' in the group wasn't easy, but to my relief they all reacted understandingly and favourably. They did not regard my inclination as a problem. To some of them it came as no surprise. Evidently the suggestion had been raised by one or two that I might be gay.

My coming out did not cause any change in the group. We carried on as usual and they treated me the same as before. Yet it made a very big difference to me. I had taken an important step by informing the group as to who I really was inside. Now I had confirmed to the outside world something I had known inside for a long time. I had grasped the nettle and immediately it eased a lot of the tension that had been mounting on the inside.

Now I had a place and an environment where I could be myself. Here I could even talk about my feelings, particularly with Margaret, one of the girls in the group. She was very open to talking with me. In fact she was one of my closest friends. She seemed to understand me. We had been good friends before and that didn't change after my coming out. Margaret had an old car and she often collected me to take me to our various sports activities or parties, as I myself did not have a driving licence. In fact we were so often together that my parents concluded that she was in love with me. I was convinced of the contrary, but appreciated her warm friendship very much. She now knew who I really was. In my innocence I concluded that once she knew of my sexual preference, a girl could never fall in love with me. That was a naïve mistake on my part.

Although I had had the courage to tell my friends at the swimming club about my sexual identity, I didn't have the guts to tell anybody else and I pleaded with them to keep quiet about the matter: 'It wasn't easy for me to tell you this and I beg you all to promise me not to tell anyone else, and above all, please don't breathe a word of this to my family.'

As real friends they kept their promise. This meant that although I had no secrets within the group, outside this circle I continued my double life. I just didn't know how to broach the subject at home. I knew I would have to, one day, but I kept putting it off. Going into the army meant being away for at least six months. After that I would consider telling my family.

In spite of the relief I experienced when informing my friends about my secret, I felt depressed. One of the reasons was undoubtedly the unreturned love. But there was more. I had taken a definite step in coming out, but still could not live with the full implications of this reality. In most circumstances I had to keep my internal alarm system in good working order. In this respect the prospect of doing military service was daunting. The army was a threatening environment to me, and here more than elsewhere I would have to be extremely careful to keep my true feelings to myself.

Another source of depression was the loss of all four of my grandparents within a period of two years. We had been very close and I saw them very often, as they lived close by. The loss of these dear relations was stunning to me. Especially with my grandad from my mother's side I had built up a warm relationship in the last year of his life. During that period he had cancer, was confined to bed and needed daily care. My grandmother had passed away a few months before, suffering with the same disease. Family members were mobilised and a roster was made for his daily care.

'Put me on for one day a week,' I told my mother.

'But you will have to cook and all that!' she objected.

'No problem. I can do that. I want to, very much. Just put me on.'

So every Monday afternoon I visited my grandfather. To be honest, the meals I cooked were basic and simple, but he appreciated my visits very much. He always tried to manipulate things in such a way that I had to stay longer than originally planned. Although he did not have a retiring disposition, neither had he been very talkative and he had never shown much emotion. Yet now I got to know a very different man. We had long and earnest conversations in which he poured out his heart. We developed a close and warm friendship and I missed him very much when he finally succumbed to the disease. This loss increased my gloomy mood.

I finally entered military life in May 1984, feeling very depressed. As expected, for my initial training as a non-commissioned officer I was billeted in the southwest of Holland, in a town called Middelburg. I felt very unhappy and completely out of place. The possibility of anything being revealed about my 'coming out' was constantly at the back of my mind. Military service is of necessity very much geared to group dynamics and I felt uneasy about being so close to other men. This situation was bound to strengthen my sense of being different, but would even more enhance my feelings of inferiority. I definitely do not have a technical bent, and this was a sure recipe for frustration and feelings of inadequacy. Weaponry is a very technical world by nature and this only served to confirm my conviction that I was not like the other men. Guns held no attraction for me as they did for many of the others. I detested both their complexity and their purpose. My reaction was that surely this proved yet again that I was not a macho type, and inwardly I felt more and more isolated.

Arriving at home on leave during the weekends, I wasn't very communicative. My parents noticed I wasn't my usual self, but could not get through to me. Instead I would withdraw to the sofa with a book to try and forget the army for a few hours. My mind was full of the bleak prospect of taking the Sunday night train back to the barracks, back to the life that made me feel so miserable. There were hardly any cheery moments during those days.

As a reaction to my depressed feelings I began to smoke joints, sometimes even when I was on duty. That was very risky, of course. As an NCO I was in direct command of a small group of soldiers. Instead of setting an example and making them toe the line, we would be smoking marijuana when on guard duty at night. To me this was a hidden expression of rebellion that gave me a feeling of satisfaction. My attitude towards the army did not really help and not surprisingly my relationship with the officers was somewhat problematic.

After six months of initial training, we were to be told where each of us would be stationed. They had announced that six of us would be sent to Germany and the rest would be placed with different units throughout Holland. Each one of us had been given the opportunity to express preferences as to our future place of service. Of course I had indicated my wish to be stationed in The Hague with an administrative unit and I was convinced that my request would be granted, because of the recommendation of the chairman of our swimming club. I was informed too that there were several vacancies in The Hague. I even had a letter from the Ministry of Defence saying that my request was being treated with priority, which had been communicated to the staff of the army base in Middelburg.

When returning from leave to the barracks for the last time, we were told that lists had been put up with our names and places of allocation. To my astonishment and alarm I found my name on the list for Germany. I had been assigned to an army base close to the East German border, a place nicknamed 'the hell' among Dutch troops. Of course I protested against this decision. What had happened to the letter from the Ministry in The Hague? 'We don't know anything about a letter,' was the abrupt answer. What about my request to be placed in an administrative unit? 'We can't make everybody happy and we cannot honour every request.'

The chairman of the swimming club had a tantrum and immediately jumped into action. The officers at my unit were angry with me about the fuss I kicked up, but in the end the decision was reversed. I did not have to go to Germany, but they refused to assign me to an administrative post in The Hague. Instead I was sent to Garderen, a regular army base in the centre of Holland, which thwarted our plans to continue my activities for the swimming club.

My eight months in Garderen were as depressing as the
first six months in Middelburg had been. Still, I learned
some valuable lessons during my time in the army. We used
to make long forced marches with full equipment. There
were moments during these exercises when I felt I had
reached the absolute limit of what my body could take. Yet
you bite the bullet and go on. You have no choice. And as
the hypnotising cadence of the heavy boots carries you
along, you realise that your body has hidden reserves of
strength you can draw on. Through this experience I
learned to push back my pain threshold, which stood me in
good stead later on in my swimming career. It taught me
not to listen to my body when I had to perform at the top of
my abilities. Perhaps this lesson also helped me through
military service.

With the same tenacity I also kept my inner life rigor-
ously hidden during the rest of my army period. The feelings were present in the background all the time, but I did
not allow them to play any role while in the military
environment.

The only pleasant spell during this gloomy period of my
life was a holiday in Tenerife while on a few weeks' leave
from the army. Margaret and I had arranged to go there
together. To me this event stood out like an oasis in a
parched landscape. While there, we met up with some
other Dutch people and had a good time together, but
although I appreciated the company, I also relished the
moments when I could withdraw to some quiet place to be
myself. I enjoyed sitting on the rocks in a beautiful spot,
looking out over the ocean, listening to the breaking of
the waves on the boulders on the shore. Here I was able

to unwind and feel at peace with myself and the world around me.

One day, as I sat in this lonely spot, I suddenly became aware of another boy, sitting a little further down. He must have been there before I noticed him. He was gazing in my direction and when I looked at him, I realised there was more to this eye contact. I felt confused. Hesitantly I looked again. In some inexplicable manner I felt I had met with a person of like feelings. He motioned me to come and join him, and I did. As it turned out he was Spanish and we couldn't really communicate verbally beyond a few words of greeting, which was all the English he knew. Yet, as if it were a matter of course, sexual contact followed nearly immediately.

This flighty and nearly anonymous sexual contact is quite common in the gay scene, but to me it was still an unexplored world and very exciting. It was as though I was sucked into the experience involuntarily, yet I desired nothing else. When I walked back to the hotel, I felt I was treading air. So this was it! It was such an overwhelming revelation to me that I had to share it with someone else, so I blurted it all out to Margaret. I was so thrilled with what had happened that I wasn't even interested in her feelings or reaction to the event. The outside world seemed irrelevant to me. I couldn't be bothered with what others thought of it. Margaret reacted as always: with understanding and sympathy. She was a real friend. It never occurred to me that the whole affair could be painful to her.

I had found what I wanted. For years I had been trying to run away from this. So often I had pleaded with God in my habitual evening prayers that he would take away those confusing and unwanted feelings. Yet he hadn't done so. If those feelings were not right, he would have taken care of them, wouldn't he? Evidently he meant me to be like this. I concluded that I should accept these homosexual feelings as a legitimate part of myself. Not only did I have to live with these feelings, from now on I *wanted* to live with them! How? I did not really know yet. I couldn't really form any concrete ideas about life as a gay. But gay I was.

6

Coming Out

Back in Holland I had a few more months of army service to complete and I still detested it as much as I had done before. Yet I also knew that on Tenerife my life had taken a turn that would be decisive for my future. However, for the time being that new direction had to wait.

On leaving the army, I returned home and went back to the job agency to find work, while in the meantime looking around for a permanent job. Of course I was very happy to pick up my sports activities in the swimming pool again and especially to be back among my friends. Soon everything seemed back to normal. Within weeks I was in full swing in the water polo competition again. I was also happy to be with my parents. Yet in spite of all this, I continued to feel depressed. At home I became more and more introverted. My parents noticed this and wondered what was amiss.

The necessity of 'coming out' at home and in my wider circle of acquaintances hung over me like a heavy threatening cloud. I needed to be able to talk with others about my true identity. Sporadically I could still talk to Margaret about my homosexual feelings, but understandably this was not her favourite topic of conversation. I sensed she'd much rather talk about light subjects and having fun.

Yet I could never function well as long as I was leading a double life. Hiding my deepest feelings became an unbearable burden and caused such tensions that I began to suffer frequently from hyperventilation – a very awkward handicap to a sportsman. Maintaining regular controlled breathing became a weak point in my swimming, and as a result I avoided competing in long-distance heats. I majored in the short distances: fill my lungs as much as possible and then just try and get to the finish as quickly as possible. Depression and inner tensions began to mount to such an extent that I decided to seek psychological help. For two years I went for counselling sessions, but I never felt they did me much good.

In 1985 I managed to find a permanent administrative job in a town near to The Hague. The office was close to the beach and whenever the weather was nice I took the opportunity to go for a walk along the seafront after working hours. Strolling along the shore I enjoyed the quiet vastness of the sea. It helped to bring peace to my restless heart.

Further along the beach was a special area reserved for nudists, but actually it was known more as a meeting place for gays. At that time I was unaware of this fact, but later on I noticed that I had developed something like a sixth sense to pick out such meeting places. One day I somehow wandered onto this section of the beach. There was a large group of boys sitting and lying on towels and sheets. I sat down a short distance away, observing the group. They were talking and having fun and there was much laughter.

At first glance they seemed an ordinary group of young people, but watching them a little more closely I realised there was a difference. These were gays! There were a few who seemed to have the word 'gay' written all over them. In fact the extravagant way in which they acted out their sexual identity was so in keeping with the stereotype mocking imitations of gays, that it disgusted me at first. I did not know the gay scene at all, yet since Tenerife I was determined to get in there somehow or other. I knew that was where my future lay.

My glances were noticed. 'Please come and join us,' they invited. I overcame my initial reservations about the conduct of some of them and joined the group. Soon I was taking part in the conversation and getting to know several of the boys. One of them, Ron, I found particularly attractive. We talked about our mutual interests and our backgrounds. He was still studying, attending a fashion college. When the group packed up, he asked me, 'Would you like to come home with me?'

'Fine,' I replied. That was the start of my first serious relationship.

Ron introduced me to the gay scene in The Hague. Although the gay life in The Hague is quite open and visible, this was a completely new world to me and I found everything very interesting. I wanted to explore this culture. It was so different from what I was used to, but after all, this was my identity.

Ron shared an apartment in town with another gay boy and there was a constant stream of gay visitors to their home. Ron introduced me to gay bars, gay discos and other gay meeting places. I must confess that I observed some of these places with mixed feelings and sometimes wondered what I had come into. It was a completely different world with a different atmosphere, and although most of the visitors were like ordinary citizens, some of them looked rather bizarre, to say the least. At times they made me laugh, but often they made me feel sad. There were old men who used all kinds of make-up to try and look young and attractive, whereas in fact they looked pathetic. *If you have to do all this when you get older, it isn't going to be fun any more,* I thought to myself.

Even so, the bars and dances Ron took me to were not the sex-oriented gay meeting places. Ron was an excellent guide to explore the gay scene with, and because I was particularly keen, he introduced me in a number of places. Yet I noticed he was a little reticent and often seemed to want to keep me away from certain places. Slowly I began to perceive the reason for this reserve. As a young and new boy on the scene, you are immediately the target of many visitors, a potential prey. I once heard someone describe such bars as a 'meat market'. Ron was evidently afraid that he might lose me quite soon if I frequented these places.

Although I enjoyed the novelty of these experiences, I also quickly made up my mind that I did not really want to spend a lot of time in the specifically gay bars. Although you will meet the odd heterosexual in gay clubs, they remain an exception. It is a very exclusive subculture and my world was broader. I did not want to confine myself to such a restricted environment. I felt more at home in the swimming pool and with my water polo mates around a table full of beer bottles. I did not want to spend too much time in dark pubs full of smoke and loud music. I decided to keep these worlds separate as much as possible.

Ron came along several times to meet my friends at the swimming club. They welcomed him and liked him, but he never took to these surroundings. All the talk revolved around swimming and water polo, which did not interest him in the slightest. Also he did not appreciate our custom of heavy drinking after a match or swimming contest. He wasn't a teetotaller, but we would swill our beer in order to get drunk and experience the coarse and senseless fun that goes with it. It made Ron feel uncomfortable. He preferred to stick to his own clubs and circle of friends.

Starting a serious relationship with Ron meant I definitely had to end my double life and come out in the open completely about my sexual identity, even at home. For days I walked around formulating in my mind how I was going to break this news to my parents. In the evening I would sit down with them in the living room and think, 'OK, this is the right moment. Now I'm going to tell them.' With clammy hands I would nervously think of the best words to start with, but time and again I found some pre- text or good excuse not to do it. Again I would postpone it to the next evening, but the next day saw a repetition of the previous evening. Yet all the time I knew I couldn't go on like this. It was impossible to hide the relationship and my family was bound to find out one day and I'd much rather tell them myself.

Finally, one evening I managed to take this formidable hurdle. As we were sitting in the living room I said, 'Mum and Dad, I need to tell you something. I have met someone and have started a relationship.'

'Well, that's great. Tell us more about her,' was their enthusiastic reaction.

'Ah . . . well, it may be a bit different from what you expect. It's not a girl, it's a boy.'

Needless to say, this bombshell took them fully by surprise. They did not know what to say. So I began to tell them about Ron: who he was, what he did, what he looked like. Of course I also told them that for some time I had known that I was homosexual. After the initial shock they reacted with much understanding and acceptance: 'This is indeed very different from what we had anticipated and it will take some time to get used to this new situation. You'll understand that. But you are our son and we love you. If this is what you are, we will love you as you are.'

I was very happy with this positive reaction. I knew my parents well enough to expect acceptance, so I had not been afraid that they would react angrily or tell me to leave the house. But even so, the immense implications of my message had made me afraid of incomprehension or grief on their part. Most likely they had entertained the happy expectation of becoming grandparents one day.

My coming out was a complete surprise to them. As it turned out, they had never guessed or noticed anything to suspect that their son had a homosexual inclination. My sister, on the other hand, reacted quite differently when I told her about my sexual preference. 'Well, I've known that for years,' she told me. To her it came as no surprise and like my parents she accepted the situation whole-heartedly.

Strangely enough I felt a little hurt by her reaction. How could she have noticed while others hadn't? I recalled the times when as a teenager my pals at the swimming club had made remarks about my appearance. Was there after all some truth in what was said? Did I really look and act differently? In retrospect I wonder how it was possible that my parents had never noticed anything that pointed in the direction of homosexuality. The most likely explanation is that they were blinded by the normal expectations that parents have with regard to their children: they grow up, they get to know someone, they get married and they have a family. Anything outside that pattern is considered a rare exception. Really, I couldn't blame my parents for not noticing my homosexual feelings. I had always been meticulous in avoiding any signal in that direction. My inner alarm system had been on guard day and night in order not to say anything that would have given me away. And if during my adolescence anybody suggested there was a feminine look about me or my legs, I certainly did not look like the stereotypical gay at this time of my life! Besides, the sports I practised were considered macho sports.

When my parents broke the news to an uncle, he reacted in utter disbelief: 'Come off it! He can't be gay. He plays water polo!'

'What has that got to do with it?' my parents retorted.

But of course in the traditional worldview that has everything to do with it. A tough sport like water polo is an occupation for 'real men', not for 'sissies'. That agrees with the old prejudice people held regarding gays. It conjures up an image of gays as fragile and feminine. If there was ever any truth in this stereotype, this image has long since lost its validity. Nowadays sports schools and fitness centres are full of homosexual men. In fact these places hold a special attraction to gays as they emphasise the physical aspect.

Shortly after telling them, I took Ron home to introduce him to my parents. They got on well and soon Ron found his place in our family. In fact, he liked coming home with me. He was accepted and also felt at home in our wider family circle. He enjoyed our family get-togethers. Perhaps he felt attracted to the stable and close family ties that he witnessed in our home.

Ron's own background was quite different. He came from a broken home with changing relationships. I accompanied Ron to meet his family, but there we had to handle everything concerning our relationship very cautiously. His family came from the West Indies and consequently he had a very different cultural background, one in which the subject of homosexuality was a taboo. Older members of the family would definitely not have understood or even tolerated our relationship, so I was introduced as just a friend.

Ron and I would often go to the meeting place on the beach where we had first met. There I got to know many other boys belonging to the gay scene of The Hague. Slowly I was beginning to feel at home in this new world.

Although we seemed to develop a serious relationship, Ron and I did not live together. At first I still lived with my parents, but when in 1986 I bought my own apartment, Ron did not move in with me, except for a few months shortly before the end of our relationship. We both had our own activities and we felt happy to keep it that way. However, as time went on our interests and activities moved further apart. Sport always remained my number one priority, whereas Ron liked to limit his activities to a small circuit of gay clubs. And although I joined him occasionally in visiting these places, I did not want to embrace that kind of life. Our relationship went on for a few years, but then slowly we started to drift apart. In the end we had to admit that we only met at home and that our household chores remained the only activities we shared together. We did an honest evaluation of our situation and decided that ending our relationship was the obvious and sensible thing to do.

Breaking up meant that after three years of being with someone I was on my own again, but to be honest I didn't mind. A new horizon had opened up. Ron had initiated me into the lore and ways of the gay culture, but a relationship had also meant restriction. Now I could go on exploring the world of homosexuality on my own without any impediments. I had begun to feel growing sexual desires that could not be satisfied because of my loyalty to Ron. Now I could experiment without having to answer to anyone for what I did. The brakes were off. I could have any number of contacts in the gay scene.

One of the first things I did was to go on holiday alone. Travelling alone meant total freedom and not having to take the wishes of others into consideration. I booked a trip to the island of Rhodes in Greece. This country attracted me enormously and here was my chance. The only drawback of a holiday on your own is the possibility of sitting down for dinner alone. I soon realised that I did not fancy that. It made me feel lonely when I had been used to having other people around me. I needed company. During the day my energy was directed at making friends. I had no trouble in contacting people, especially gays, and in truth my main aim in making friends was sexual contact. Before going on holiday I had enquired within my circle of gay friends about gay meeting places on Rhodes. I did not know then, but found out later, that there are gay travel agencies with catalogues that tell you exactly where to find such places. Going to Rhodes for the first time I still had to do most of the searching myself. Yet my sixth sense for scenting out gay bars and hang-outs seemed to develop well and I did not lack contacts.

I began a new relationship with one of my new acquaintances on Rhodes. As he lived on the island, I went back there three times within one year. He came over to Holland once. In Greece homosexuality is a controversial issue. When visiting my friend's family, we had to mask our relationship and present it as a normal friendship, just as I had done with Ron's family. I am quite sure that everybody in the house perceived the true nature of our friendship, but that was absolutely not to be named or hinted at. It wasn't supposed to exist within the family. They would have fought tooth and nail any suggestion made in that direction.

In the end a relationship at a distance does not work, so a year and six months later I finished it. There was absolutely no fidelity in our relationship on either side. Deep in my heart I did not even want such a restriction. I began to learn that there is a common duplicity in most gay relationships. You hope for fidelity on the part of your partner, and your ideal is an exclusive sexual relationship, but reality is vastly different. In my experience most gay relationships are flighty and without obligation. You need one another, but at the same time you don't.

My team mates in the water polo and the swimming club continued to be my closest friends. Every weekend after the match we would go out together. They had accepted the fact that I was gay, but this was seldom alluded to. We drank together, talked together, laughed together and sought new experiences together. We were fascinated by occult matters and even dabbled in occult activities and games, trying to contact the unseen world. There was a period in which we preferred to go to occult horror films. Some of these were very extreme and obscene. I decorated the door of my apartment with a very large poster of Pinhead, a hideous character in the film *Hellraiser*. It was shocking for any visitors knocking on my door to be welcomed by this ghastly figure with nails protruding from his head, staring at them. Their shocked expressions gave me a kick. Quite in keeping with this extreme culture, we also experimented with psychedelic drugs, cocktails of all kinds and combining alcohol and marijuana.

Although conversation often revolved around occult subjects, spiritualistic occurrences and demon activity, the subject of God and faith in him was a no-go area. One of my friends was a fanatic atheist and did not appreciate any serious talk about God. My vague religious notions were tolerated, but these were just about all he could take. The others did not care to talk about God and were not interested in talking about religion, with the exception of Olga.

Olga was engaged to Frans, one of my friends in the group. She had a clear conviction on Christianity and went to a reformed church regularly. Frans grew up in a Catholic family, but didn't practise any religion. I had a desire to know more about God, and after discovering Olga's religious interests I often had long and serious conversations with her. She was surprised to meet someone in this godless and worldly group who wanted to talk about God. We became good friends and I was best man at their wedding. For many years she continued to be my link with religion, with Christianity, even after she and Frans were married. Invariably, whenever we met, the conversation would turn to God and faith, and although Olga's religious notions were more philosophical than personal, these talks kept me awake to the fact that there was more between heaven and earth than just the blue sky. Deep inside me there was something that longed for God. It was a half-conscious but at the same time deep desire. It seemed so contrary to the life I was living, but I was not aware of the paradox. I worked hard, swam hard and drank hard, but even when I stumbled up the stairs in the small hours of the morning, after a wild night of drinking and feasting, with a large amount of alcohol rushing through my veins and my brain completely fuddled, I would still kneel down by my bedside before turning in. I would say a prayer as I had been used to for so many years. Deep inside, there was a conviction that this was important, though I couldn't explain why.

7

Dave

One of the highlights in the Dutch calendar is the holiday of 30th April, commonly known as 'Queen's Day', the day we celebrate our queen's birthday. Towns and villages are decorated orange, the colour of our royal family, and everywhere there are fairs, open-air games, children's processions and open-air concerts. Together with some friends from the gay scene I had arranged to spend that day in Amsterdam. On the 30th April Amsterdam is usually flooded with hundreds of thousands from all over the country.

It was a lovely spring day when we boarded the train. Ron was also with the party. The train was absolutely packed with people headed for the same destination and with the same purpose of partaking in the festivities in the capital city. In spite of the fact that we stood cramped together like sardines, the mood on the train was festive and jocular. People were dressed for the occasion, some wearing festive or extravagant clothes and many with orange hats or other orange accessories.

Once in Amsterdam we started on a trail from pub to

pub, seeking out particularly the many gay bars in that city. I did not know the gay scene in Amsterdam very well, but Ron was quite at home there and introduced me to many people. One of those he introduced me to was Dave. We met him when our party had literally squeezed into the bar Amstel Taveerne, a well-known location close to the River Amstel. The place was so crowded that once inside you could be lifted from your feet without falling down. I couldn't move an inch, and found myself looking into the face of Dave. His striking features made me curious to get to know him and as we couldn't move anyway, we struck up a conversation. We soon found out that we had a major common interest: sports. Dave had been an athlete for many years and at one time he had come close to qualifying for the Olympic Games for England. I was fascinated by this man and I soon learned that he was a well-known figure in Amsterdam. He worked as a photographic model and also did catwalk modelling for the fashion industry. There was chemistry between us and we arranged to meet again.

This new friendship led to all kinds of new developments and new areas to be explored. As Dave's Dutch was rather limited, we conversed in English. Dave had come from London to work in Amsterdam. He was English, but his ancestors came from the West Indies. Yet that was as much as he knew about his roots, since he had never known his father and had grown up outside his family. In fact, Dave was very reticent about his childhood, which I gathered had not been a very happy one.

Because of my visits to Dave, I now regularly travelled to Amsterdam and fell in love with that city. Dave had an apartment in a splendid old mansion close to the city's beautiful Concert Hall, right in the cultural heart of the capital. His rooms looked out on the main art museums of Amsterdam: the Municipal museum and the Van Gogh museum, as well as the Rijksmuseum, famous for its Rembrandt collection. I relished the pleasant atmosphere of the Museum Square and the beautiful and stately mansions around it. At Dave's I met all kinds of interesting people from the art scene and the fashion world. This was all new to me and very exciting.

But most of all I was attracted to the person of Dave himself. During my years in the gay scene I had met numerous men, but never had I met someone to whom I felt so strongly drawn as I did to Dave. Never before had I met someone who roused in me the thought: 'I'd like to spend the rest of my life with this person.' Yet with Dave this was exactly what I felt. I wondered why he held such appeal to me. He was so different. Our lifestyle and contexts were poles apart.

As a model Dave had a very busy professional life. When talking of models, one generally imagines perfect looking men and women, meticulously dressed. Strangely enough, that did not apply to Dave at first sight. He was photogenic, to be sure, but his appearance in daily life was eccentric, and that is putting it mildly. A few times I went along to photo sessions and to one or two of his appearances on the catwalk. It was an interesting experience to get to know this world from the inside, but I noticed a lot of sham and superficiality. It did not appeal to me and I was glad I did not have to spend a lot of time there. Dave moved easily in that world, not because he liked it, but because it was his way of making a living. I soon noticed he just played the game as a born actor. In private he was a completely different man.

Dave made a lot of money in his profession, but he did not live a luxurious or extravagant life. That wasn't his style. On the contrary, outside the catwalk or the studio I never saw him wear designer clothes. He went around in odd pieces of clothing, often second-hand stuff that he fancied and had picked up somewhere. He put on the weirdest combinations. He would wear socks of different colours, for instance, and a beret full of safety pins. He had numerous rings in his ears. Yet he certainly did not look effeminate. I would rather describe him as 'exotic'. He was a bit of a maverick in his professional environment and did not care a hoot for the etiquette and decorum peculiar to the fashion world. In his daily contact with people he was cheerful and superficial, but the few who really got to know him perceived that deep inside there was pain – hidden sorrow from the past. There were secrets he kept buried within himself, invisible to the outside world. He was exuberant on the outside, but inside there was a silent cry for real love.

A month after we got to know each other, Dave left for England to do a few weeks of fashion shows. When he came back he wasn't feeling at all well. At first we thought he had eaten something that did not agree with him, food poisoning perhaps, but as it got worse, he was sent to hospital for tests. The results were devastating: HIV-positive.

The first action he took was to inform me. He wanted us to face reality. 'Look, Richard, I think it would be better to end our relationship. We both know what these results mean. It may be a few months or a few years, but the end will be the same. I will die of this disease. That is not a good basis for a budding relationship.'

But I wasn't ready to accept this conclusion yet. All kinds of conflicting thoughts were rushing through my head, but not the thought of giving up our relationship. Especially now, with this bleak prospect, I did not want to abandon Dave. We had started a relationship and I felt that we should stick together now the going was to be tough.

All of a sudden the spectre of AIDS changed from an ever-present threat you did not want to think about into a stark reality. The thought of this dark invisible menace, in which we'd rather not believe but couldn't deny either, could not be pushed away any more. At times I anxiously wondered whether I had contracted the disease. However, my contact with Dave had been without risk up to that point and the possibility of being infected through him was very unlikely.

At this stage of our relationship we did not live together, for practical reasons. Most of Dave's work was in Amsterdam and I still worked in The Hague. We travelled a lot between the two cities in order to be together. I often stayed with him, but he also came to my place in Voorburg. That same summer I invited him to come and meet my parents. As I was rather worried how they would react to his unorthodox apparel, I had begged him to have some consideration for them: 'Dave, as it's the first time you are going to meet them, please go easy on them and mind what you wear.' I had explained how to get to my parents' house and had instructed him to come in through the garden, as the back door was always open. On that memorable day there was a knock on the back door and in came Dave.

Oh my goodness. . . . I thought. He wore an old and worn boiler suit, the legs turned up halfway up his calves. Underneath he sported two different socks in colours strong enough to make your eyes water. His feet were placed in large floppy shoes. He wore his beret with the golden safety pins and other paraphernalia attached to it. A colourful handkerchief was tied to one of the straps of the boiler suit and odd bits and pieces were added elsewhere. I could see he had made a brave attempt at complying with my request to be sober in his appearance. Some of the more extravagant accessories had been left out and the bigger earrings were missing. But in all, his attire contained enough unorthodox elements to jolt the unwary passer-by. Dave did not dress so exotically in order to be conspicuous. This was how he was.

Of course I had prepared my parents carefully, but still I admired the composure with which they took in this drama of eccentric dress. They had got used to the unconventional figures that I took home, but they had all looked dull in comparison with Dave.

I presented him to my parents, and my father introduced himself as Piet Oostrum. 'Hi, Pete,' was the hearty response from Dave as he reached out his hand. This was too much for me. I did not know where to look. Feelings of shame made me wish that the earth would open and swallow me up! How were my parents going to take this?

I should not have worried. The intonation with which Dave spoke his greeting was so innocent and disarming that my parents sensed the genuineness. They responded in like manner and greeted him without reserve. Dave on his part quickly noticed that he was accepted as he was.

Still, there must have been a moment when my father wondered what had come over them now. He must have had his doubts, even though he put a brave face on it. It must have pained him at times to see his son attaching himself to such unorthodox figures. But my mother and father got on well with Dave. The friendliness, the warmth of their uncomplicated hospitality and the cosiness of our home were like an oasis to Dave. He wallowed in it. He simply loved to come to my parents' house and in the course of time it became the place he preferred to be – drinking tea with my mother, chatting, telling stories to my dad, endlessly talking. He plunged himself into it as though he were trying to catch up on something important that had been lacking in his own life. This was an answer to his inner cry for love and belonging. In my parents he found something he had never known but had always desperately yearned for. They simply gave him the loving parental attention that he had missed as a child. He had finally come home. And I admired the capacity of my parents to love.

I did not want to add to the shock of introducing Dave by informing my parents that he was HIV-positive, at least not for the time being. I told Dave that in due course we would have to tell them, but Dave was adamantly opposed to informing them about his physical condition. As time went on I realised that the main reason for not wanting to reveal his condition was a deep-seated fear that they wouldn't want to have him around any more once they knew. He didn't want to lose the warm and welcoming home he had found. Yet how long would we be able to keep this secret?

Two months after Dave was diagnosed as HIV-positive, he came down with pneumonia and was taken to hospital in

Amsterdam. He was in bad shape. For three weeks nearly every day I travelled the 40 miles from The Hague to Amsterdam to visit him. It was a hectic time. I had my job and my sports activities, but I wanted to support Dave as much as I could. It was also a difficult time emotionally. If ever Dave needed me, it was during such periods of severe illness, but it worried me to go through the ward where he lay. It was a section for AIDS patients and at that time it was nearly exclusively occupied by men from the gay scene. It was a frightening experience. During those days our lives revolved entirely around the sickness, the hospital, visits, and discussions about the needed medication. Dave was prescribed a whole arsenal of medicines.

At last the pneumonia was conquered and Dave was discharged from hospital. He seemed to pick up again after some weeks and on first sight there did not seem to be anything amiss. At such moments I tried to dismiss the reality of the disease from my mind – ignore it in fact. I reckon this was a form of self-preservation. It was emotionally exhausting to constantly think about his illness and the consequences.

Dave went back to work, although he adapted his schedule and activities to the new circumstances. He limited the amount of work he did. As a model he worked on contract for agencies and photographers, so he was free to accept or turn down any requests. Financially he was in a position that meant even quitting work altogether was an option. However, that was not his choice, as it would have been a signal that he was giving in to his illness.

To the outside world everything seemed to be back to normal, but our lives developed a radically different pattern. We lived in fact from one manifestation of the disease to the next. Gradually more physical defects emerged: malfunctioning of organs, infections in the mouth and even skin cancer. Some of these were a real handicap in his work as a model.

We lived for the good moments, when the problems seemed to ease off. We tried to enjoy such short periods intensely. And together we struggled and fought our way through the increasingly frequent periods of hospitalisation and intense treatments.

As I was very close to my parents and my sister, I found it very hard to keep quiet about Dave's condition. Constantly I had to be on my guard not to say a wrong word and reveal the true nature of his problems. It put me in a predicament. I said to him, 'Dave, I do understand your unwillingness to inform my parents about your illness, but I can't live with this hide-and-seek situation any more. Please let me at least share our problem with my sister. I must have someone I can talk to about my fears and concerns, and I know I can trust her not to tell my parents.'

Dave agreed, but in the end even he had to face the fact that my parents had to be informed. His good periods were shorter all the time and the spells in hospital longer. His strength was wearing out, which was becoming alarmingly visible. New problems occurred, such as partial facial paralysis. Work became impossible. At the same time he would come to Voorburg more often than before in search of rest, peace and loving care.

After a year it was obvious we could not hide the truth any longer, so I said to him, 'Look, Dave, we have to involve my parents in this. They see you so often and they cannot but notice that there is something very wrong with your health. It was difficult enough to get them to swallow the fact that you spent three weeks in hospital just for a bout of pneumonia. Normally that never happens. They realise you are in and out of hospital and are beginning to wonder what is happening. How can we explain all the new ailments and illnesses? We cannot go on finding excuses.' The stories of AIDS patients being rejected and thrown out by their community or family frightened Dave, but he also realised we could put this off no longer.

He shouldn't have worried. My parents were shocked when they heard the news, but not because of fear. Their concern was for Dave and immediately they took over part of the care that had fallen to me. This was a great relief to me, because not only did it give me moments to relax but also a place to share my anxieties and worries.

Naturally I did not have much time to go around with other friends during those days. Life had taken a different turn. The only distraction I had was the swimming pool, which continued to be an important part of my life. I had heard of a gay swimming club and decided to contact them. They invited me to join them whenever I could, so I did. As a trainer within my own swimming club, I couldn't help giving them some instructions when visiting them one day in the swimming pool. Evidently they needed some help and my advice was much appreciated. They asked me to join them as their trainer and coach. However, I had decided that I did not want to get involved in more sports activities, as Dave's condition required me to be at home as much as possible. I should have been wiser than to give some instructions voluntarily. I always found it hard to say no to people and did not want to disappoint them by turning them down completely, so I promised to help them out with a limited amount of initial training.

Inevitably I ended up as trainer for their club. During the training sessions they told me about the Gay Games, the global sports event for the gay movement, which would be held in the summer of 1994 in New York. Immediately I was excited. That was something I would love to be part of. Taking part was not difficult as there were no qualifying matches or limits. My times were actually quite good and I was regularly training anyway, so I decided to put my name down and go for it, though it meant extra activities. There were meetings and instruction sessions for the Dutch participants. All kinds of preparations were to be made and I was soon fully involved.

In the meantime Dave's condition deteriorated. We went from one crisis to the next. He was increasingly in need of care. Other measures had to be taken. Two years after the first signs of the disease, Dave left his house in Amsterdam and moved in with me. Initially that helped to alleviate the burden. He longed for a safe and quiet home. Here I could care for him. I did not have to travel to Amsterdam any more and Dave was spared the frequent tiring journeys to Voorburg, where he preferred to be anyway.

He needed help with a number of things. At one stage a 'portacath' – portable catheter – had to be placed under his chest for the direct application of medicines. He had previously gone to hospital frequently to be put on a drip to get his medicines, but now these drugs could be administered at home. As he was unable to do this himself, I had to help him.

More and more he was limited in what he could do. In the end he was confined to bed. From the beginning we had known that there was no hope. Now Dave had resigned himself to this fate and he did not seem to have any desire to fight it. I guess the reason for this was his disappointment with a life in which he had lacked the most important thing: the love of parents and the safety of a home. When at last he had found what he had yearned for, a family that at least to some extent could fill that void in his heart, the dreaded disease put paid to this. That was the final blow. He gave up and passively waited for the end, tired of life.

Dave accepted the fact that it was all over and wanted to discuss the funeral arrangements with me. Though we never spoke about faith or God, I noticed he had something of a religious notion. As we talked about his choice of music during the funeral, he said he wanted the song 'To my Father's house' by the Les Humphrey Singers to be played. You don't choose a gospel song from the seventies just because it sounds good. Somewhere deep inside Dave there was a longing for a house and a Father better than those he had known here on earth. Years later I often think back to this moment with much regret and pain. What a pity that I did not have anything to give him at that crucial moment. Every night I would kneel down to say my prayers, and of course I prayed for him too, but even though we lived together, Dave never knew about these prayers. I did not really know the God I addressed my prayers to and I had no idea how to introduce this Great Unknown Person to Dave.

Dave's illness raised a lot of questions in my mind about God. Confronted with his imminent death, I began to think about what would come after, but my thinking did not go beyond the common vague religious notions that people often express when confronted with the death of a loved one. Dave was a good guy, so I was pretty sure he would go to heaven. He loved others, and was good to them. In fact, he did not do at all badly in his life on earth. Besides, he had had a very difficult youth, lacking the normal blessings of childhood, which wasn't fair, so I reckoned he really deserved something better after this life. These were the criteria on which I based my convictions. It gave me a sense of peace in the face of his approaching departure from this life.

During the last phase of Dave's illness many of his bodily functions failed. In the end the disease also affected his brain. A dementia set in which made communication very difficult, and during the last week of his life no contact was possible. The last months were a very difficult time for me. Dave was restless at night and needed constant attention. Sometimes I did not sleep at all for several nights in a row. I began to show signs of exhaustion.

One Saturday night my team was to play a water polo match and I asked my parents to come to my house and take over from me to watch over Dave. I had reached my limit emotionally and just needed a break for a few hours. Swimming always helped me to unwind and forget my worries and anxieties for a while. On the way home after the match, the thought struck me that Dave might not be alive any more. As I arrived, my parents told me that he had passed away five minutes earlier: Saturday night, the 5th March. Dave's demise was a loss, but did not come as a surprise. I was sad, exhausted but also relieved.

Dave and I had arranged the funeral in detail beforehand. If he had had his own way, the burial would have taken place with only my family present. To him this was his family. He did not want his death made known by putting a notice in the newspaper. And above all he did not want a funeral with special attention to AIDS victims and AIDS, though he did donate a large sum of money to a nursing home for AIDS patients.

Though I respected his wishes, I remonstrated with him against the idea of not letting his old friends and colleagues know about his funeral. An announcement in the newspaper and cards to a limited number of acquaintances was the least we should do. He had been a popular figure and so many people in Amsterdam knew him and would wonder why they never saw him any more. They had a right to know what had happened. Dave had reluctantly agreed.

The funeral was attended by my family and a few friends from the swimming club. Some mutual friends from the gay scene turned up, but hardly anyone from the fashion world came. Dave's half-sister from England came over with her son to be present at the funeral. She was the only family member with whom Dave had had contact. He had always avoided any mention of his family background, but he had told me about this half-sister. She and her son stayed with me for a few days and gave me a glimpse into his background. The day after the funeral she said: 'Richard, I have got to tell you something. It concerns Dave's age. He was much older than he told you and others.'

When going through his papers after his death, we had not been able to find a birth certificate, but we did find out that he was not registered in the Netherlands and had actually been living and working there illegally for twelve years. According to my information Dave was born in 1957. His sister told me he was twelve years older. 'If he had revealed his true age, they would not have accepted him as a model,' she explained. In England, where he had also worked as a model, he had asked his sister never to reveal his true age.

I found this hard to believe. He had always looked so young, but perhaps that was partly due to the way he dressed. In fact he had looked so young that some people thought he was younger than I. When I later told all this to the surgeon who had treated him in hospital, he did not want to believe it either: 'Believe me, I have treated many people and I know what the skin of someone of his age looks like. He wasn't a day older.'

However, his half-sister was right, as we soon found out. Hidden in the cover of one of his books we did in the end find Dave's personal papers, including a birth certificate.

Finding out this truth upset me at first. I felt cheated. We went through so much together; we spent three very difficult years sharing our lives. How could he have hidden from me such a basic fact about himself right up to the end, even in these circumstances? However, as I thought about it, I could smile. This was Dave's humour. Yet at the same time it showed the tragic reality of his life. What other secrets went to the grave with this boisterous and extravagant man? He had lived a life in the limelight. His face and figure had illustrated many magazines. He had been at home in a world of glamour and glitter. He was well known in the gay scene. But who had really known him?

After the funeral, two good friends of Dave, called Henri and Charles, noticed how drawn and pale I looked, and were worried. They said, 'Richard, you look completely done in. When all the hassle of the funeral is over, you must take a

break. We intend to book rooms in a hotel on the island of
Terschelling and we want to take you there for a few days.'
I was both physically and mentally at my end, so I agreed.

A few days later they came to collect me and together we
drove the 130 miles to the north of Holland to take the ferry
to the lovely North Sea island of Terschelling, with its
beautiful beach and sand dunes. Swimming or sunbathing
was of course impossible as it was the middle of March and
rather cold and windy, but I enjoyed every minute of walking on the beach, even in stormy weather and rain. All the
tension and stress of the past months seemed to blow away
as I leaned against the wind and felt the sand hit my face.

Henri and Charles lived together in Amsterdam and had
a steady relationship. They had known Dave for years and
together we talked about him. This was a great comfort to
me. Henri came from a solid Christian background. He
talked about religion, and my longing for God and spiritual
things was roused again. He evidently took his faith seriously. Henri was a very good-natured and steady guy with
a positive outlook on life. I admired him. To me he served
as an example. *So this is what it means to be a Christian*, I
thought. He combined his gay lifestyle with his faith.
Together with Charles he attended a church in Amsterdam.
Now I had found someone I could talk to about spiritual
matters – someone to whom I could go with my questions.
And questions I had in abundance, my religious notions
being as muddled as they were. I loved talking with them
about these things, though I must say I received very few
answers. But there was a growing longing in my heart for
something more, something deeper, something I couldn't
exactly define yet. What was life all about?

8

Gay Games

The short holiday had been refreshing, but returning to my apartment was like stepping back into emptiness. For three years I had known that Dave wouldn't live long and his death hadn't come as a surprise. We had had ample opportunity to say farewell. Yet it affected me deeply. I missed him.

At the same time I felt a great relief. A burden had been lifted. The past months had been trying. Now I could sleep again and I could get on with life. It opened a new perspective, but at the same time it was hard to find my feet again and fill the void that Dave had left behind. For the past two years my daily schedule and most of my activities had been dictated by caring for him. Now I needed a new orientation and I felt at a loss. I had thought that, as we were prepared so well for his passing away, I would get over it quickly. But I was wrong. In fact I seemed to live in a denial of the pain I felt inside. I was running away from it. At first I tried to drown out the empty feeling by throwing myself head over heels into the nightlife of the gay scene. I looked for comfort and companionship in contacts and sex, but nothing seemed to still my aching heart. Somehow I had to find a new incentive and a new motivation for my life.

Dave had urged me to participate in the Gay Games, whatever his situation. He had very much wanted me to prepare well and be part of that event, not just for myself but also for him. At least here was something I could turn my attention to, also in honour of him. I realised I only had a few more months to prepare. Exhausted as I was because of the many sleepless nights and the physically and emotionally difficult task of nursing Dave, I was not in good shape and I knew I had to work hard in training for the Games. So I shifted my attention to swimming again, as well as to the meetings and preparations with the 200-strong Dutch delegation that would go to New York. There was a host of practical matters to be attended to: tickets, correspondence, documents and the presentation of the delegation. Probably in reaction to my sorrow, I threw myself too fanatically into all these preparations, with the result of injuring my shoulder during training. Tired and worn out as I was, I should have gradually increased my training load rather than going at it so frantically. Yet I was determined not to miss the Games and I continued training as much as my shoulder allowed.

Then came the great day and I left for Amsterdam airport to fly to New York. It wasn't difficult to pick out the other participants who were travelling that same day. The Dutch organisation had issued a training suit specially designed for our delegation by a well-known fashion designer. The many red, white and blue suits were easy to spot in the departure lounge. A feeling of euphoria came over me. All of a sudden I realised I was going to be part of an historic event. The gay movement was gaining momentum in many Western countries and we were going to show the world that we were to be reckoned with! Added to this was the thrill of going to America and especially New York. For many of us who had not been there before, these names had a magical ring to them.

Getting off the plane in New York, we got into cabs to drive to our various destinations. Each one of us had received a document containing all travel information, as well as an address where we would be billeted for the duration of the Games. Most foreign participants would be staying as guests in private homes rather than in hotels.

I shared a cab with two other Dutch athletes and we had to be dropped off at different addresses. The ride into town made a deep impression on me. It was my first experience of New York and as we drove from the airport in the direction of the city suddenly we saw the well-known bridge and the island of Manhattan looming up ahead, with that magnificent skyline of skyscrapers. So often we had seen these sights on TV or in magazines. The thrill of actually driving into it gave me goose pimples. Driving a short distance through Harlem felt like passing through a movie. TV series and films had made the scenery so familiar to us.

Both my fellow passengers were delivered to their respective addresses. I was lucky to be the last one and have the treat of an extra long ride through the city. I had given the driver the note with the address and after a while I anxiously started to wonder whether he could find it. 'Do you know the address?' I enquired. The look he returned said enough. Evidently I had insulted him. His reply was loud and clear. How could he *not* know such an address?

We turned in the direction of Central Park South. I was of course absolutely ignorant as to what kind of area this was, but soon it dawned on me that we were heading for one of the poshest and richest suburbs of New York. That was where my host lived and where I was going to spend the ten days of the Gay Games.

The driver pulled up in front of an impressive building with a red carpet on the pavement in front of the entrance and a canopy above it. 'Here you are!' he said.

I stepped out onto the red carpet, feeling completely out of place. The weather was hot and I was perspiring all over, even though I had taken off all excess clothing and was wearing just a sports vest. I was met by a man in black tails, with golden buttons and a top hat. He took my suitcase from the cab and led me to the entrance. I glanced over my scant and sweaty attire, but did not get the chance to improve my appearance because I was announced and ushered into a lift, which swiftly took me to the eighteenth floor. Moments later I stepped into a luxurious apartment and was welcomed by my host. He was an older man who in the past had been a swimmer himself. He had preferred to have a swimmer as a guest and he quickly made me feel at ease. For years he had worked as a model in the fashion world, evidently earning a lot of money. Now he was vice-president of a well-known fashion company. As I soon learned, New Yorkers are open, direct and active. True to type he did not allow me much time to relax. 'Unpack your luggage and take a bath. Then we can go outside and I'll show you the area.'

I surrendered to the circumstances. I took a quick shower, changed into clean clothes and shortly afterwards we were outside. I was walking as in a dream. The change from the modest environment of Holland to the grandeur of Manhattan had been abrupt. Jetlag gave me an eerie feeling of unreality as we walked along Central Park and into the streets of Manhattan. Involuntarily I kept looking up at the immensely high buildings. My host told me that everyone who visits New York for the first time feels inclined to do that. He was an excellent guide and gave me lots of information about the buildings we passed, mentioning names and companies, many of them connected to his profession and often sounding familiar because of all I had learned from Dave.

In the ten days that followed, my host took me to several posh parties, in penthouses or on rooftops, where I met people from the fashion industry and the world of the arts, some of them well known and all of them well off. To me this was like visiting another planet. I felt like a complete stranger, just like Peter Sellers in *The Party*. But like him, I enjoyed moving between these people even without knowing any of them. I did not really want to get to know this world either. Through Dave I had had a glimpse of this same culture back in Holland and had decided it wasn't for me. I had witnessed how superficial it could be. Yet I enjoyed observing the people, and being able to eat caviar on toast at will was a rewarding experience.

However, I had not come to New York for parties. The day after our arrival the great opening ceremony of the Gay Games was held in the big baseball stadium in the Bronx. We were escorted to the stadium in groups, as it was not safe to go there on our own, and this was a new experience too. This seemed so incredibly unreal to someone from Holland.

The opening ceremony was a magnificent event. There we stood, thousands of athletes from all over the world, in formations according to country. As each country was announced, the respective team marched into the stadium, welcomed by tens of thousands of spectators. When it was our turn, we marched in, dressed in our red, white and blue training suits, and each one of us opened an orange-coloured umbrella as we entered. We marched through the stadium like an orange wave, featuring our Dutch national-ity. But much stronger than the national pride, we felt another pride: the gay pride. Here we celebrated a different unity – the unity of the gay community throughout the world. Each time a team was announced from a country where gays were still being persecuted or marginalised, the cheering and applause was twice as loud in support of those who had dared to nail their colours to the mast and come to the Gay Games, openly identifying themselves as gay and defying the public opinion back home. For Americans and West Europeans this openness and freedom is taken for granted, but for others who do not know this freedom, arriving at the Games was like a liberation and a welcome to the family. Here within the confines of the stadium they could be themselves and feel absolutely safe. Here were only gays and you did not have to mind your p's and q's. You could be open about your sexual identity without any fear of negative repercussions. As the applause sounded we realised we were fighting for a common goal and making history; putting the gay movement on the world scene.

The next day the Games began in earnest. All competi-tions and contests took place in different locations on the island of Manhattan. That meant a lot of travelling to and fro. I had put my name down for the 50-metre butterfly stroke, 50-metre freestyle, 100-metre freestyle and 100-metre medley. There were races every day and I simply loved to hang around in the swimming pool. I did not want to miss anything.

Occasionally I took a short break from the warm and moist atmosphere of the swimming arena and wandered through New York or Central Park in order to get away from the noise and excitement and be by myself. It was midsummer and the weather was glorious. As I felt the sun shining on me and reflected on the experience of these Games, I felt at peace with the world and myself.

The atmosphere during the contests was terrific. The swimming was very competitive, but the sense of unity always predominated. I did not win any medals. I was classed in the age group that contained swimmers who performed on a level close to the world's best. There were several who had won medals at the Olympic Games. Besides, my shoulder injury was playing up again. But in these Games, participating was much more important than winning. The show of solidarity was the overriding aim, which actually came closer to the original Olympic ideal than the nationalistic competition we witness at the Olympic Games nowadays.

In spite of my painful shoulder I enjoyed the swimming, as I always do. In the setting of the swimming pool I became oblivious to the fact that this was a gay competition in which, by its very nature, the homosexual identity was central. In any swimming contest, regular or gay, sexuality never played any part for me. In this environment the only thing that counted was the sport. I was completely focused on the coming heat, the starting shot, the swimming, the finish, and how I had performed. Of course I met many friends there in the swimming pool, but my focus was never on sexual aspects; it was exclusively on the sport.

In addition to the sports events, there were many other activities organised as part of the Gay Games. In the evenings there were feasts and parties everywhere. We did not have to organise anything ourselves, but could just choose from a wide variety of activities that were offered. Many parties were organised around a theme. Within the gay movement there are numerous subcultures, such as the 'leather scene' and transvestites. We could choose between small parties and large feasts, but there were also cultural events, parades, art exhibitions, concerts and even church services. The common factor was that all these activities emphasised and confirmed the gay identity.

The ten days of the Games went by like a dream. It was one big party, the highlight being the closing ceremony in the Yankee Stadium. This magnificent sports arena was packed with a wildly enthusiastic crowd of 70,000 people, all of whom you had something in common with: your sexual identity.

Outside the stadium the country teams stood waiting in formation again, this time to march in for the last time. There was a sense of nervous anticipation. The adrenaline pumped through our veins. The signal was given and suddenly we started marching through the gate and into the impressive stadium. The experience was so overwhelming that I did not know whether I was asleep or awake. I was carried along with it. It was as though we merged into one huge collective consciousness. We seemed to experience this great moment as one and in complete unity.

I had not won any prizes, just like thousands of the other athletes, but together we had won and we marched in triumph. The world could not ignore us any more. And I was part of this entity. Here I belonged. This was me. This was also the message I wanted to preach to the world, the cause I wanted to serve. It became a gigantic demonstration of our solidarity and our right to exist. No cost had been spared to get the message across.

On the plane back to Holland, the closing ceremony still echoed in my head. I thought about all I had seen and heard, and remembered particularly the thrill I felt when the announcement was made: 'See you in Amsterdam in four years' time.' We were going to host the next Games. I felt the excitement run down my spine. I was determined to be involved and not just as an athlete. I wanted to be in the thick of it. I wanted to promote those Games like an advocate and an evangelist. Those Games were going to preach the gay message – if possible even more powerfully than in New York. And could you think of a better location than Amsterdam, the gay capital of Europe? In New York I had received my calling. As the aeroplane touched down on the runway of Amsterdam airport, I knew my mission.

9

Addiction and Attraction

Back in Holland I immediately looked for ways of preparing for the Gay Games in 1998 and of course I focused my attention mainly on the swimming activities. First of all I expanded my activities for the gay swimming club. I wanted to promote the Games, encourage gay sportsmen to take part and it was my vision to come to those Games with a swimming team that was really well prepared. Feverishly I set to work. Apart from the zeal for the Gay Games, there was another unconscious motivation that drove me on to work hard at these preparations: all the busy activities helped to push out any thought of Dave.

'You haven't yet got over the loss of Dave,' my parents noted with growing concern, as they saw me throwing myself like a madman into all these activities.

'Oh yes I have,' I replied. 'We said our goodbyes so often before he died. There is nothing to worry about on that score.'

But they were right. Dave was still very much on my mind and I tried to flee from that reality by frantically directing all my energy and attention to other things, hardly allowing myself any moments to reflect or to recognise my grief. I was running from reality.

Besides the sports activities I developed another pattern of escape. Increasingly I submerged myself in the gay clubs and gay nightlife. Of course there weren't any impediments now. I was a 'bachelor' again. Living on my own I did not have to answer to anyone for what I did or what hours I kept. At night I went around all the gay bars in The Hague up to closing time. Then I would find a few friends and move to a gay club or other club where gays met. I developed a lifestyle that wasn't particularly healthy and profitable for a sportsman, but I seemed to be unable to stop myself. The emotional tension rose and I was inevitably heading for a breakdown.

Then in November of that same year I collapsed. I could not cope with my grief any longer. I spiralled downwards in depression and tried to numb the pain and the dark thoughts by giving myself over to sex, marijuana and very large quantities of alcohol. More and more I began to crave for sexual contacts. I yearned for affection and physical touch. But just caressing did not satisfy my longings. It had to end in sexual contact. In the end this became a compulsive daily pattern that I couldn't break out of. Actually, I did not want to. I wasn't interested in relationships. I just wanted to satisfy my lusts. I couldn't live any more without these short moments of indulging my sexual cravings.

Not all my contacts were safe. My recent experience had taught me so well what terrible consequences such conduct could have for myself and others, but in my depression it seemed that I couldn't care less, and I shut my eyes to this fact. I was rapidly getting addicted.

The combination of sports and an intensive nightlife, including the consumption of much alcohol, seemed a sure recipe for failure. Yet strangely enough I was able to combine my wild living with a good show in the water polo competition, and the friends at the swimming club were still very important to me. Olga, Frans's wife, continued to be a comfort to me during those difficult days. We often talked, and invariably the conversation turned to God, though on a rather superficial level. I reckon I did not really want deep conversations on that subject at that time. What I needed was someone to listen without scepticism when I talked of my secret prayers; someone who would be interested and sympathetic when I spoke of my inner unrest and dissatisfaction.

My depression deepened and began to affect my performance at work. I lost interest in what I was doing. My work seemed so pointless. Life became a tunnel without light at the end. Why did I bother? When alone at home I would indulge in self-pity. I would play records that made me feel blue. Endlessly I repeated 'Come and go with me to my Father's house' and the music of Chopin, which at Dave's request had been played at his funeral. Only then the tears would come. At such moments I desperately wanted to shout out loud to give expression to the pain inside, but no cry would come out. It felt as if the grief in me was growing physically, filling me up but not being able to find a way out. Slowly the tension built up and there wasn't a safety valve to ease the pressure. All kinds of irrational fears popped up in my mind. I did not feel safe any more in my own house. Maybe there was too much that reminded me of Dave.

At the office I told my colleagues that I was thinking of quitting everything and moving to Amsterdam. For some time I had been playing with the idea of settling in Amsterdam, partly because of the coming Gay Games and partly because I liked the place, but I had been reluctant to give up all my securities. Now I wondered whether moving to Amsterdam could take away my depression and gloomy thoughts. I loved Amsterdam and felt at home there. I still remembered very vividly the first time I went to that city all alone. I recalled how I walked out of the Central Station onto the street that leads to the Dam Square. I just loved the scenery, but above all the atmosphere. It felt as though Amsterdam enveloped me like a comfortable blanket. It shut me in its arms and I had been in love with that city ever since. It held a magical sway over me and not just because of its gay scene and tolerance. That first time I seemed to have a premonition that one day I would live there and find my life's task and purpose in that city.

I decided to begin moving my social life to Amsterdam. Henri and Charles, the friends who had taken care of me after Dave's funeral, lived in a beautiful house along a canal in the inner city. They offered me the use of a small room, where I could stay at the weekends. On Fridays I would take my luggage with me to the office and at the end of the day I would travel straight from work to Amsterdam. Arriving at Henri and Charles's, I would throw my luggage in a corner and step out again. The gay pubs were just around the corner and I would submerge myself in the nightly gay scene of Amsterdam. There I gave myself over to my uncontrollable desire for sex. In the small hours of the morning I would stumble in again, benumbed and nearly unconscious through the large intake of alcohol, drag myself upstairs, try to say my prayers at my bedside and fall asleep.

Yet the more I sought satisfaction through the wild life I was living, the larger the emotional void inside me seemed to grow. And the more I tried to drown my depression, the deeper the bouts of depression became. The many flighty sexual contacts did nothing to take away the emptiness inside. But what else could? I tried starting a relationship again, but it didn't work. I met Harry. Our relationship lasted four months. Then we broke up, though continuing to meet as very good friends.

The end of the relationship with Harry helped me to make a decision. I finally resolved to settle in Amsterdam. To some of my friends this move was incomprehensible.

'For goodness' sake, why do you want to live in this city, of all places?' one of them asked me. 'What do you expect to find here?'

'I feel safe here. I feel at home and so welcome,' was my reply, but I saw both astonishment and cynicism written all over his face. He couldn't imagine anyone coming to Amsterdam with such expectations.

'If there is loneliness anywhere, it is in Amsterdam. Many people come and crowd this city in search of heaven knows what, but it is a crowd of lonely people,' he said cryptically.

A few years later I would recognise the truth in his words, but even so, I still kept feeling at home in this city. Deep inside, something seemed to confirm that this was the place for me. I sold my house in Voorburg, quit my job in The Hague, found another job closer to Amsterdam and in

January 1996 I temporarily moved in with Henri and Charles. A deep wish had come true and with this change it seemed as though suddenly there was light again at the end of the tunnel.

I recall how I used to get up early in the morning, walk the little distance along the quiet canal and wait for the streetcar at the stop on the bridge, as the first sunlight penetrated the haze that hung above the water. The quiet beauty of this scenery gave me a feeling of inner peace, a sense of having arrived home. In such moments the murky mist of my depression seemed to lift. Amsterdam filled up the emptiness inside to some extent.

After five months with Henri and Charles I managed to get my own apartment. Now I had settled for good in Amsterdam and it gave me a feeling of accomplishment.

The move to Amsterdam brought about several other major changes. I quit the water polo team and said goodbye to my old mates at the swimming club with whom I had shared so many years in close friendship. During the first few months we kept in touch regularly, but soon I found new friends and activities in Amsterdam, and slowly most of the old friendships faded. Over the years Frans and Olga were the only two I stayed in contact with.

In Amsterdam I joined the gay swimming club Thermos Havana. There I met Ronald. He was as fanatic a swimmer as I was and we became very close friends. We never developed a relationship. It was a purely platonic friendship, but he was perhaps the best friend I ever had. We understood each other, supported each other and did many things together. Of course I got to know many people in the gay scene in Amsterdam and made many acquaintances, with or without sexual contact, but my friendship with Ronald rose way beyond that level.

Together we took part in many gay swimming competitions and had a lot of fun. We were both involved in the preparations for the Gay Games '98 and worked hard towards this goal in training as well as in creativity. We did a lot to promote the Games during international gay swimming events.

After the break-up of my relationship with Harry, I had definitely decided never to try and start a steady relationship again. Occasionally I met someone with whom a relationship seemed to begin, but it never lasted. I did not really want it, as this would curtail my freedom too much. A relationship involved a certain amount of fidelity, even though this tended to be a rather relative concept in the gay scene in which I moved. Friendships were much more convenient to me.

I continued to visit Harry regularly, but for a very different reason than sex. We had something else in common. Harry was very much concerned with questions about God and the Bible. He was evidently seeking to know the deeper truths about these subjects and I had the same desire. We both felt the emptiness of the kind of life we were leading and we were searching for answers. But Harry had an advantage over me in that he seemed to know a lot about the Bible. I sensed my needs, but was fumbling for the answers, which seemed to evade me every time I felt I was coming close to the truth. Instinctively I felt Harry could help me to discover something important. The way he talked about religion was so different from the more general conversations I had with Olga and some others. Harry's words contained a new element. His notions of God and religion were not vague. They were not limited to a misty New Age-like religious feeling. Harry was much more specific and concrete. He had inside knowledge of the Bible and believed that what was written there was absolutely true. From Harry I understood that believing in God can never be done in a non-committal way. Relating to God seemed to imply an unconditional commitment to him, although Harry himself seemed unsure whether he would be willing to make this commitment.

Harry even suggested that the homosexual lifestyle was against God's will. He evidently was at odds with himself about this aspect. I could not follow him here and I ignored this part of his belief. Harry lived in the gay scene, just like I did. He did the same things I did. How then could he say that homosexuality was not God's plan and purpose for a man's life?

'But how can you reconcile these beliefs with the fact that you live as a gay?' was my reaction.

'I find it hard not to live like this, but I don't feel happy about it. I do not have peace about it,' Harry explained.

I did not know what to make of this, so I dropped this part of the discussion. I definitely wanted more specific knowledge of God, but the aspect of my gay identity was an established fact as far as I was concerned. I *knew* I was gay. I had known for years now and my family and friends had accepted it. Years earlier it had cost me a lot of emotional energy to accept my sexual identity and I was not going to go through a process like that again. In the past I had pleaded with God to take those homosexual feelings away. He hadn't done so and for me that was ample evidence and confirmation that God meant me to be gay and approved of it.

Yet all the other things Harry told me about God and the Bible fascinated me increasingly. I was convinced that he was talking about the God to whom I prayed each night. Yet with this admission a feeling of uncertainty began to creep in. My very simple prayer had over the years developed into a drone, half-consciously rattled off each night out of habit. Such a prayer seemed out of proportion to the greatness of God that the Bible showed. Was a prayer like mine allowed? Wasn't it rather a hypocritical prayer? Sexually I lived a licentious life. I was convinced that there wasn't anything wrong with a homosexual relationship, but even so I realised that my dissipated sex life was far from right. I didn't need the Bible or the church to convince me on that score. I had also noticed that my lifestyle had had an adverse effect on my prayers. They had deteriorated from an earnest child's prayer to a mere recited standard formula, which mainly focused on my own interests. I had to confess that by now I did not even have the expectation that my prayer went beyond the ceiling. As I questioned myself I had to admit that I was faithfully saying my prayers only because of a feeling of solidarity with my childhood. To me it was the prayer of a hypocrite and this made me feel very uncomfortable, but I did not dare to give it up. I needed to find out more. I wondered about getting hold of a Bible and finding out for myself. However, I did not have the foggiest idea where to get a copy of the Bible.

One summer day in 1996 I went to a large department store in the centre of town. In the book department I looked for the category of religion in search of a Bible, wondering whether a store like this would sell such an unusual book. To my amazement there was a whole range of Bibles in all kinds of shapes and versions. The price tags were rather daunting. I wanted a Bible, but did not want to spend too much money on it. After all, I wasn't absolutely sure yet that it would deliver the answers I was looking for. In the end I bought the Old Testament and the New Testament in two separate books, as that turned out to be the most economic option. I was oblivious to the fact that one was a Protestant version and the other a Catholic one. Even if someone had pointed this out to me, the difference would have eluded me. I wasn't even aware of the fact that there were numerous translations. To me a Bible was a Bible. I began to read.

Shortly afterwards I went on holiday to Sitges in Spain with a number of friends from the gay scene. (Sitges is one of the popular holiday resorts for gays in Europe.) I had put my New Testament in my luggage, as I was determined not to interrupt my search for the truth. During the day we spent our time in the sun on the beach and in the sea. Towards the evening we went to the hotel to rest for an hour before jumping into the hectic nightlife of Sitges. During that hour of rest I would lie on my bed and read the Bible, going through the Gospel of Matthew. The others noticed it, but did not mind. Many in the group had some religious interest, mainly of a vague New Age variety, but I considered that a convenient kind of religiosity, as everything fits into it and it doesn't require a clear commitment. I could not be satisfied any more with foggy religious notions. I wanted something more solid and searched for real answers. After all, I was searching for the truth about the God to whom I had prayed for many years. I really wanted to get to know about him now.

My friends noticed how seriously I applied myself to my quest. Some pulled my leg about my devotion; others showed a mild interest and sometimes talked a little with me on the subject. However, no one ever spoke about our homosexual identity in relation to the Bible.

Reading the Bible opened a new world to me and it got hold of me, though I absolutely did not fathom the depth of what I was reading. How could I without someone to explain the words to me? My hunger to understand these words grew every day, as did my desire to talk about them and discuss the meaning of this message for my own life.

It was an odd mixture of activities. When after reading for an hour I closed my New Testament, I would get up and go to the night clubs and bars, where I would look for the sexual fulfilment without which I could not live any more.

With Ronald I could talk about everything and he was also open to discussing the major questions of life with me, but even with him the conversation would halt at the moment my queries became specific. Whenever I zoomed in on Christianity or a specific matter of the Bible, Ronald would change the subject and steer the conversation to a more superficial level. That did not satisfy me. I wanted more. I knew something had to change in my life.

I felt hunted by my own desires. On the one hand there was the constant and uncontrollable craving for sexual experience and on the other there was the yearning for another kind of life. What kind of life that should be, I did not know yet, but I did know it had to do with God. More and more I felt torn apart inside, being pulled to and fro by these conflicting desires. I became increasingly dissatisfied with the life I was living. How long would I be able to keep this up? I felt that I was heading for a crisis I could not avert and to which I seemed to be driven involuntarily.

In the autumn I went to London with some colleagues from work. Before leaving, I had made sure to get some addresses of gay bars and clubs in order to be able to organise my contacts. In the evenings, when my colleagues headed out to the pubs, I took my map of London and set out for the gay scene. My colleagues all knew of my preference and did not mind.

One evening, crossing Trafalgar Square, I spotted a group of young people singing. I noticed they were some kind of evangelists and immediately I was fascinated. They were handing out flyers with the words 'Jesus is Alive' and they were talking about the Bible. That was my subject, so I stopped to listen to what they had to say. Here at last was a chance to get to know more about the Bible. I drank in every word they said and felt a deep longing in my heart for more. I was ready for it. Slowly I gathered courage and edged my way forward between the other listeners. I wanted to hear clearly what the speaker was saying, but also wanted to be noticed by these people. I had a strong desire to talk to one of them. I observed the dynamics of the group and noticed that they moved through the crowd in order to strike up a conversation with anyone interested.

If they are so set upon talking to people, it will not be difficult to get their attention and have one of them come and speak to me, I thought to myself, while I tried to look as interested as possible. *Here I am! Please talk to me!* I tried to communicate. In the end I found myself right in front of the speaker, but it seemed as though he was looking straight through me, without seeing me. Nobody spoke to me. Not one of them even offered me a flyer! Longing to receive something, I picked one up from the street, which had been discarded by another passer-by.

The group finished their activity, packed up and left. I stuck the flyer in my passport and, feeling deeply disappointed, went on my way. I desperately wanted to know more about God and here there were people who wanted to talk about him, but nothing had happened. Why did God not answer the cry from my heart? The empty feeling inside increased, and so did the longing to have this emptiness filled.

To every rejection, disappointment or depression I always responded by immediately searching for a sexual contact. Over the past few years, that had become my method of compensating for any dissatisfaction or discrepancy in my life. Like the drug addict would take his drugs and the alcoholic would turn to his booze, I compulsively fled to sex. Walking away from Trafalgar Square I headed straight for a sauna where I knew I could get what I wanted. It wasn't difficult. Once inside I soon met someone with a similar aim. Later on that evening we sat talking together for a long time. It turned out he was an actor playing a major role in the musical *Jesus Christ Superstar*. I was awed when he told me, not so much because of the role he played, but because of the coincidence of meeting someone from that musical and getting into a conversation about Jesus Christ. It seemed an unlikely place for a conversation about spiritual things and it concerned a musical of a very dubious spiritual nature, which of course at that time I did not realise, yet it was uncanny how many little incidents somehow linked me to the message of the Bible. Time and again I was confronted with something about God. Yet although he seemed to pursue me, every time I wanted to take hold of him, he seemed to evade me. And with each disappointment, my longing to find him increased. More than ever I became convinced that only God could fill the void in my life and satisfy my deepest desires.

Back from London, I had only two days to pack my suitcases again. This time I travelled with Ronald and a Dutch swimming team to Montreal for an international gay swimming competition. The event was organised in the splendid swimming stadium of Montreal that had been built especially for the Olympic Games of 1976. In my opinion it is the most beautiful swimming stadium ever designed. The citizens of Montreal probably look at it with mixed feelings, as I heard one of them comment that 20 years after the event, they were still paying taxes to cover the costs. To me it was a great experience to be able to swim in this special place. I enjoyed every minute of it and for a few days I forgot all my inner unrest and questions.

A fixed part of the programme at these gay swimming events was always the closing ceremony, the 'Pink Flamingo', with a comical or bizarre presentation by each of the national teams. These were short theatrical pieces, mostly rather nonsensical, but always something with colourful costumes and very creative. It was the first time a Dutch team had taken part in this particular event and we had decided we wanted to present something special and impressive that would really represent Holland – something as Dutch as clogs and windmills. I had taken a lot of initiative in organising our show and we had prepared most of the elaborate accoutrements back home in Holland. Our presentation consisted of a twelve-foot-high figure with a portrait of our queen on top. Nearly the entire Dutch team was concealed underneath the wide royal garment. We were all dressed in traditional local costumes and wooden shoes. The 'queen' was ushered in to the slave march from *Aida*. Once inside, the figure suddenly exploded as we came out from underneath to perform a traditional clog dance. The presentation ended as the whole group jumped fully dressed into the water for a final swimming act. The piece caused great hilarity, and to me it was the highlight of the event and a moment in which all depression and bad feelings seemed to disappear.

However, arriving back in Amsterdam at the end of October, I also returned to my feelings of dissatisfaction and discontentment with my life. I went back to my job again, where things went from bad to worse; back also to the compulsive pattern of visiting gay clubs in search of sexual satisfaction; back to a lifestyle that could best be described as addiction; back also to my worrying thoughts that something in my life was wrong, very wrong, certainly in the light of my search for God. The life I was leading was slowly destroying me. How long could I go on like this?

It was a grey autumn day early in November. As I did so often, I walked through the Marnix Street in Amsterdam towards the day sauna in a narrow side street. I was on my way to this gay meeting place, seeking a sexual contact to satisfy my insatiable heart. But that same heart was restless.

All of a sudden something pulled at me from behind. It felt as though there were cords attached to me, which jerked me back. The sensation was so real that I looked over my shoulder involuntarily, though at the same time convinced that there wouldn't be anything to see. I knew there was nothing attached to my back or grabbing me from behind, yet the experience was so real and disturbing that I needed confirmation. For a moment I thought I was losing my mind. *What's happening? Am I going crazy? Am I finally cracking up through all the worrying and thinking of these past months?*

Yet the moment these thoughts crossed my mind, I realised that there was a completely different cause. I was flooded with the conviction that it was God who had stopped me in my tracks! He himself was there to stop me. The thought overwhelmed me, but I knew it to be absolutely true. God was showing me in an undeniably clear manner that I should not go on. I should not go to the sauna and I should not do what I had planned to do.

I turned around and went home, never to walk the old path again.

10

Home at Last

I went home still deeply awed by the experience of meeting God. I knew that was what had happened. There wasn't a shadow of doubt any more in my mind. For many years my relationship with God had been a one-way street – at least that was how I had experienced it. I had faithfully said my prayers. I believed he heard me, but I had never witnessed a direct answer to my prayers. Or maybe I should say that I had never recognised anything as a direct answer from God. Except perhaps his silence, as for instance when I had begged him to take away my homosexual feelings.

Now he had stepped in very emphatically, just at a time when I was beginning to think that my prayers could not go beyond the ceiling. His intervention was so real that I had sensed it physically. He had spoken without any words, but the message was loud and clear. I could not deny the reality of my experience and I acted upon it. As I did, my heart was flooded with a deep sense of peace.

Strangely enough, my decision also gave me a feeling of victory. Never had my search for sexual contact been a matter of 'succumbing' to cravings. I did it only too willingly. I had never wanted anything else. I had known no alternative. Now I had taken the first step, surprisingly the old craving for sex did not seem important. There was no battle; there were no desires to put down or fight against.

The confrontation with God filled me with a very different desire. Now more than ever I wanted to get to know him. I wanted to find out more about him, much more than the small pieces of information I had gleaned from reading the Bible, which I found hard to understand anyway. My craving turned to God and to ways of getting to know him.

As I wondered what to do next, it crossed my mind that the most likely place to turn to in search of God would be the church. Yet that posed a problem. I did not really have any knowledge of churches, apart from the fact that I had become aware that there were different kinds of churches. Yet what distinguished one from the other was quite beyond me. I had seen broadcasts of church services on the local television channel of Amsterdam. The TV station had an information page with addresses of these churches. More or less at random I picked out the name of one I had seen: the Congregation of Christians. When later on in the week I met Harry, I mentioned it to him. Maybe he could advise me.

'The Congregation of Christians? Oh, I happened to visit there last week. They're OK, but not really my style. You could give it a try. Perhaps it'll suit you.'

Harry's words gave me courage. Going to a church was a very big step to take. I had literally only been to church twice: once for a funeral and once for a wedding. But the strong longing in my heart for more of God overcame the reluctance I felt at crossing the threshold to this strange new world. And so on Sunday I actually made my way to the church.

It was a very different world indeed, and I did not feel at all comfortable as I walked in. The surroundings and the culture seemed to be light years removed from my own reality. The small church hall was already partially filled as I made my way over the aisle. Somewhere in the middle there were a few unoccupied pews and as I was afraid to sit down too close to the other churchgoers, it felt safe to sit down there. I wondered how I was supposed to act and what I should do. Would people notice that I did not belong here? What would they think? I was nervous and felt a knot in my stomach. Would the service last long? The pre-conceived idea I held about church services was that they must be boring and monotonous, and to be honest I had entered with the expectation that the service would not be very appealing. However, as the music and singing started, it was lively and attractive – very different from what I had occasionally watched on TV. This took me unawares and confused me. On the one hand I had come here because I was looking for something important. On the other hand I had stepped inside with a silent hope that my prejudices about this strange world would be confirmed. That would have given me the excuse to walk away again and say, 'I have tried it, but as I expected, church does not have anything to offer me.'

The whole service was rather relaxed, which in fact made *me* feel ill at ease. All my recent tensions and unrest seemed to well up inside me. And as often happened whenever I

was under pressure or very nervous, I started to hyper-
ventilate, which only increased my uneasiness, as I was
sure I was drawing attention to myself. *As soon as the service
is over, I'll make a beeline for the door*, I promised myself,
hoping it would be over sooner rather than later.

After quite a lot of singing, the preacher got up to
speak. I listened, but a great deal of what he said was
beyond me.

I sighed a deep sigh of relief when the service was over. I
got up from the pew and tried to move as quickly as possible
to the door. The church members were evidently not in a
hurry, as coffee was being served in the back and most stood
around to greet one another and chat. Working my way
through the congregation, I was nearly at the door and
ready to escape when an older lady addressed me: 'Hi, I've
never seen you here before. Are you visiting for the first
time? Would you like a cup of coffee?'

To reject such a friendly invitation to a cup of coffee
would have been rude, and as there was nobody waiting at
home, I did not have a good excuse to say no.

'My name is Corry,' the lady introduced herself and she
went on to ask me who I was and where I came from. I've
never found it hard to answer such questions and I told her
quite frankly and openly about my life. The gay scene fea-
tured prominently in my presentation of myself and I gave
Corry a vivid picture of my life with my friends. To someone unfamiliar with the gay scene, my descriptions must
have been a bit shocking, but it wasn't my intention to upset
the lady. It was my normal manner of speaking about these
things. I often made use of such occasions to preach the
message of gay emancipation, as if I were an evangelist of

the gay movement. I felt called to put our case to anyone ignorant of the gay lifestyle or wanting to understand us, whether it was at work, with family or in a church I'd walked into for the first time in my life.

Corry listened quietly to the glowing report of my life and my praises of the gay scene. Not once did she interrupt or question what I said. When I finally dried up, she asked me what I thought of the service and the sermon. The preacher had spoken on chapter 4 of the book of Revelation – not a particularly good passage to start with when you do not know much about the Bible. Most of the sermon had been lost on me, but looking back I do not think it would have mattered whether the preacher had spoken on the Gospel of John or Leviticus. The result would have been the same. It was God who had an appointment with me that day in church.

'Do you believe in God?' Corry asked. Sure I did. I told her that I prayed every evening and that I had done so since I was a kid. The patient lady then began to explain the gospel to me in very clear and simple terms. She explained who Jesus was, what he had done for us when he died on the cross. She made it clear to me that he suffered and died for me; that he had taken the punishment and the guilt of my sins upon himself, so that I could be forgiven.

'Did you know that?' she questioned me.

'No, not really,' I had to confess. All those years I had concluded my prayers by saying '. . . in the name of Jesus Christ, amen', but the meaning of this expression had been a mystery to me. I had never understood the role of Jesus in the Bible story. Of course I was very familiar with his name, as unfortunately it is so often used as a common curse. And I had seen his figure in the cradle in Christmas scenes and on the cross as a crucifix. Yet if anyone had asked me the meaning of Easter, I would never have been able to explain it. My knowledge of the Christian faith was quickly exhausted. What Corry told me was all new to me, and it affected me deeply.

'Do you believe that the Lord Jesus Christ is the Son of God who died for you on the cross and wants to forgive your sins?'

'Yes, I believe that,' I answered, as deep inside there was the conviction that he had indeed done so.

'What you need to do, is to say that to God in prayer,' she went on. 'Would you like to do so now, together?'

This invitation came as a bit of a surprise, but I decided that since I had taken the big step of going to church, I might as well go the whole nine yards and say a prayer. So we sat down to pray together. My prayers at home had always been a very personal thing, carried out in my own way. I had no idea how to do that in these surroundings. But Corry led me into a prayer. She taught me phrase by phrase how I could express myself to God. She taught me the well-known sinners' prayer. I confessed to God that I was a sinner and needed his forgiveness. I thanked him for the offer of Jesus Christ, and for his forgiveness. I asked him to renew my life. Though it was a simple prayer, as I spoke it out I was sincere and meant it.

After finishing the prayer, we had another cup of coffee and then I left, stepping out of that strange new world back into the familiar surroundings of Amsterdam, trying to fathom all that had happened. It seemed so unreal and yet so true and good.

The week following my first visit to church I experienced a sense of peace in my life that I had not known for
a long time. Strangely enough I did not immediately connect this peace to the experience in the church and the
prayer with Corry. I had felt uneasy during the service
itself and rather out of place in the congregation. Yet the
next Sunday I decided to go to this church at least once
more.

'How was your week?' Corry had collared me immediately after the service was over.

'Well, you wouldn't believe it,' I said, 'but I felt really
good this week and I didn't go to a pub even once.' To some
faithful church members, not going to the pub might sound
obvious, but to me it had meant breaking through a pattern
of life that had become second nature. It had been an
unearthly experience: no sex for a whole week and no getting drunk!

Later on, when looking back to that week, it hit me
what an amazing change had taken place. From the first
time I visited the church, my life of addiction was interrupted and since then there never has been any 'old style'
sexual contact. Something powerful was at work in my
life, but I wasn't fully aware yet of the magnitude of the
change that was taking place. I also did not realise the
implications this change would have. The only thing I
knew was that I had not had any sexual contacts and that
contrary to what I would have expected, this abstinence
felt good – very good indeed. Something else had taken its
place, but I did not yet recognise this something else. I did
not yet understand what God could do in the life of a
human being. I hadn't heard yet of the Holy Spirit whom

God gives to anyone who repents and turns to Jesus Christ for salvation.

I told Corry that I had stayed at home all week and had felt an inner peace. She smiled and said, 'I think we have to go one step further.' She began to explain that when we confess our sins to God and believe that Jesus Christ died for our sins in order to restore our relationship with God, he sends the Holy Spirit into our life to begin a work of renewal. He wants to change us into the person God meant us to be. 'You see, Richard, the Holy Spirit is at work in you and he is the one who can give you peace and rest.'

Slowly it began to dawn on me what had happened during the past week. Corry took her time to explain to me more about a life with God and I was eagerly taking it in. As we discussed various aspects of my life, we reached the subject of my sexual identity. The previous Sunday I had extensively informed her about my life in the gay scene and she knew my position on this.

'Richard, you told me that you read the Bible. We believe that the Bible is the word of God, in which God reveals to us who he is and who we are. In the Bible he tells us why he has made us and how we should live on his earth. The Bible also clearly states that God created human kind as man and wife, and he showed us his purpose in doing so. You told me about your homosexual life and what that means, but I do think that God had another plan when he created man and wife. What do you think about that?'

Under normal circumstances I would have got up now, raised my voice and aggressively demanded full acceptance of homosexuality. Such conduct wasn't in my nature, but it was part of the defence mechanism I had built up over the years, whenever I met with any doubt about the legitimacy of my homosexual lifestyle. People had to accept me completely as I was, and if someone questioned that, I had always used strong verbal means to make them change their mind. A week earlier Corry's words would have sounded outrageous to me. But instead of my usual reflexes, and to my own utter astonishment, I heard myself say, 'Yes, I believe that's true.'

Immediately there was something inside me that rebelled. *But you can't say that! It's a complete denial of who you really are.* Yet deep inside I also sensed that what I had just said was true.

If you check the psychology books, they will probably tell you that by agreeing with Corry's statements, I should have instantly dropped into the deepest identity crisis without hope of ever recovering from it. But that didn't happen. On the contrary, I will never forget the week that followed. Each evening as I returned home from work, I would take my Bible and read. I drank in the words. My understanding was still limited, but I noticed the words had a new meaning to me. I felt intensely happy. Often I would find myself kneeling, with my hands lifted up, thanking God, feeling as though I was enveloped in a cloud within which everything else blurred and only he mattered. I was so full of love for God that I just had to sing, although my repertoire was very limited. I had only half picked up two or three songs in the two church services I had been to. I did not even remember all the lyrics and had no songbook. I did not know very well how to praise and thank God, but with the little I had, I set to work. I simply had to, as my heart was overflowing. Those days were like heaven on earth to me. I knew and experienced that God was there and he was so precious to me. How this was possible, I did not know and I did not care. I just knew and only wished that time would stop and I would never know anything else but this experience. I was a different man and God was so close.

Naïvely I thought that everyone in the church experienced God in this way every day. Afterwards I found out that this was not the case. That realisation does not reflect on the other believers, as though there is something wrong with them, but it rather shows my ignorance about life with God. For many, that moment of first love lies way back in the past, but I was still right in the middle of it. And the experience was so powerful that at times I wondered whether I could take any more.

During those days, God's presence was so real to me that it seemed as if I was taken up into a different dimension, which shut out everything else. It felt like living in two mutually exclusive worlds. During the day I worked at the office, but in fact I was still not performing very well. I fulfilled my tasks, but my work did not really interest me. I lived for the love of God, day and night. I spent many hours on my knees, confessing the many things that had gone wrong in my life and the sins I had committed. For some time it had begun to dawn on me that the wild and promiscuous life I had lived – even apart from my sexual preference – had not really made me a happy man. It had been harmful to others and to myself. It had been consuming me. I had grown dissatisfied and disgusted with my own lifestyle and I had thought that it would take years to reverse my course. But now it was happening as if by a miracle.

I had not been prepared for such a powerful touch of God. All the filth and shame came out in big waves. It felt like a major clean-up inside. I was constantly cleaning up things that God brought to my mind, often in tears and always with a deep sense of repentance and sorrow over what I had done. It surprised me. Where did this feeling come from? In the past I had never thought of any of these things as bad. At worst I had considered them to be faults, mistakes or inconveniences. Now, somehow or other, God showed me that, though he loved me greatly, he hated the things I had done. And I realised that I had done these things against *him*. This conviction brought much emotion and many tears. But there was also unspeakable joy, as each step in this process of cleansing was invariably followed by a sense of deliverance and freedom. God was making everything new. These were very important and precious moments to me. I was deeply impressed as I watched him at work in my life. This was his doing. My knowledge of God was still very scanty. He was the Great Unknown, but he had revealed himself to me on a very intimate level and I had said yes to him. He had come so close. This was the best place to be. Whatever else was to happen in my life, I now knew I had finally arrived home.

In 1994 in the Yankee Stadium I had thought that I knew who I was and I had found the family where I belonged. I had felt confirmed in my homosexual identity. Now I knew better. I had found something immeasurably greater and better. I had always proclaimed that I was gay, but now

I knew that this wasn't how God looked at me. Certainly, there are realities in my life that have to do with homo-sexuality, but that doesn't form my identity. Now I had arrived at the place where I belonged: home with the Father, who showed me my true identity. I was his child!

11

First Love

The experience of God's love was so overwhelming that I wanted to tell everybody, but words could never fully convey the feeling inside me. Two weeks after my conversion, I visited my parents. I wanted them to be able to share in the joy I was experiencing. It all seemed so simple and straightforward: you pray to God, you confess your sins, you ask him to fill your life and subsequently you will experience something you have never known before. How could I not want everybody else to share this feast?

As soon as I entered the house I blurted out: 'I have found Jesus Christ and my life has completely changed. God has made me so happy.' I told them about my experience with God. I tried to explain what that meant, but it was difficult to express the wonderful reality of meeting God, however hard I tried. I also told them about my new approach to my sexual identity. This was not something I wanted to shout from the rooftops, but it was an important element in my new life. God had changed my life so radically and I had to inform them, so I said, 'I am also convinced that God has shown me that I am very different from what

I have always told myself I was. My identity is not in my sexuality. I have found my identity in the fact that God loves me as a child of his. I am not gay. That is not how God meant a man to live.'

The glowing report of my conversion was quite a mouthful for my parents to swallow, but when I told them I had come to the conclusion I wasn't gay, they protested. For over twelve years I had preached the message of my homosexual identity. I had told them in detail what that meant and how I felt. My statement that in fact the contrary was true hit them like a bombshell. For a few moments they were speechless. As usual, my mother was the first to react: 'Just wait a moment, Richard. If you are trying out Christianity and it makes you feel good, well, that's great for you. We have no objection. But don't forget you *are* gay.'

Her reaction floored me. I was so impressed with what God was doing in my life that I had fully expected my parents to say something like: 'That sounds great! We would love to experience the same.' Of course, my expectation was naïve. I realised that when my excitement died down. In fact, their reaction was so understandable. The news came very suddenly and the change was abrupt. For anyone who has never experienced God or has not been yearning for him, such an experience seems weird and confusing. My parents looked at my religious interests with suspicion. It all sounded so radical and extreme. They were convinced I had ended up in some creepy cult that had brainwashed and confused me.

To me, on the other hand, darkness and confusion had lifted. I relished my new life, but above all the love of God.

I started to look forward to church services with delight: not only the Sunday service, but the Friday evening prayer meeting as well. I wanted to be involved, and not having much else to contribute, I began by helping in practical work, such as setting up the sound system for the services. But above all, I was hungry for God and had an insatiable thirst for his word. I began going to the Bible study evenings. They had just started a new series on the apostle Paul's letter to the Ephesians. This Bible book was explained in great detail, and although there were still things I did not understand, these studies helped me greatly in comprehending the basics of the gospel of Jesus Christ.

There was another new Christian in the congregation who, like me, had experienced a radical change and had the same hunger for the word of God. Together we attended Bible studies by several well-known Dutch Bible teachers in a town in the centre of Holland. We went from one service to the next. I bought books, tapes and CDs with sermons. I wanted to know everything. What did the Bible say about the meaning of life? For what purpose are we here on earth? What does the future hold? Slowly, many questions were answered and many blanks in my mind were filled in.

Corry, the lady who had so graciously helped me during my first visits to the church, advised me to seek help concerning questions around my sexual identity. 'Richard, it's important that you get some professional counselling with regard to your sexuality, but we are a small congregation and do not have anyone able or qualified to help you in this matter. I have an address of an evangelical organisation that specifically counsels people in this field. Do contact them,' she said as she handed me a note with the phone number of 'Different'.[1]

Different is a ministry helping people who wrestle with problems of sexual brokenness, such as homosexuality. In my encounter with God it had become very clear to me that homosexual relationships are not in accordance with God's will and purpose. This inner conviction was something God himself had put in my heart. My own knowledge of the Bible was too limited to base this conviction on. Although I wasn't convinced I needed any help, I contacted Different and a week later I had a first talk with Johan van de Sluis, the man who had been leading this ministry for 25 years and who himself had been gay.

Johan invited me to come for seven counselling sessions. After that I could take part in group sessions, which in turn would be followed by participating in a support group. The total course would take two and a half years. I nearly fell off my chair in amazement. Surely all this was rather unnecessary! These past few weeks, so many things had changed so radically, and I had had such wonderful experiences, that homosexuality was not a problem any more. I had left the old life behind, hadn't I?

Johan explained that anyone living in homosexuality as long as I had would have recurring feelings in that direction for at least four or five years. I was flabbergasted. *Surely*, I thought, *a few talks and explanations of what God's word teaches on that score will be sufficient for me.*

However, as a recently converted Christian, I decided to follow the advice given, and soon enough I discovered that

---

[1] For further information on Different visit www.totheildesvolks.nl

Johan had not exaggerated. The talks with him helped me to understand my own feelings and gave me insight into how to interpret and handle them in my new life with God. My life had radically changed indeed, and God had replaced the old life with a new life, but it soon proved true that it generally takes years for this change to have its full effect on certain aspects of our lives.

My initial reaction to Johan's information was not strange, because the first few months after my conversion I did not experience any sexual temptation or longing for sex whatsoever. It was as though sexuality had disappeared from my life altogether. Of course it hadn't, as I was to find out in due course. I was still human. But in his grace God gave me a break. It did not really require any effort on my part not to pay attention to sexual matters, not even when meeting old friends.

Of course I did meet old friends regularly. Although my focus had shifted from the gay scene and pubs to a life with God and to churchgoing, I still lived in Amsterdam, where I had been accustomed to a busy social life and a wide circle of friends. Not long after my conversion, I faced my first dilemma. Some months earlier I had put my name down for a gay swimming competition in Frankfurt, Germany, in December of that same year. What was I to do? Was it right or wise to participate? For the first time in that initial period of heaven on earth, I felt uncertain and at a loss as to what to do. My question was: 'What does God want me to do?' I knew I had been converted and many things were changing in my life, but what was wrong with sports? I was a swimmer to the core. Yet I knew it wouldn't be helpful to go into a situation where I would be exclusively with old friends.

Such events provided more than ample opportunity for temptation. On the other hand, I was supposed to take part and not doing so might give the impression that I did not want to associate with my friends any more. Could I let them down? And I did like my sport, didn't I? I felt confused and torn apart.

As I was arguing within myself, I picked up my Bible, which lay open at the second letter of the apostle Peter, the book I was studying at that time. As I glanced at it, the seventeenth verse of chapter 3 caught my eye. Here the apostle counsels us to be on our guard, as we know where the dangers are. *I know exactly where the danger lies*, I thought. *I have made a clear decision. I know what to avoid, so I can be on my guard*. I concluded that I could go to Frankfurt.

In retrospect I think that if I had asked anyone for advice, they would have strongly dissuaded me from going. I would now do the same if anyone came to me for advice on a similar matter.

However, a few days later I drove to Frankfurt, together with three other members of our gay swimming club. Those guys didn't know what had hit them. All the way from Amsterdam to Frankfurt I kept telling them about the gospel. I had a captive audience for five hours and was determined to make them share my experience. I was full of joy and I just couldn't stop. I also told them that I had discovered that gay sex was not what God had meant for us. Those guys had most likely anticipated a more comfortable journey!

I did not feel any inhibition or shame in sharing the gospel and the truth about my change. This was partly due to my innocence and lack of knowledge as far as the Bible and Christianity were concerned. But I did not care, and they listened. Even if they had made fun of me, which they didn't, I wouldn't have stopped. I had discovered a precious truth and I was not going to keep this treasure to myself.

We arrived in Frankfurt and all our attention was taken up by the sport and the coming competition. Sex never played an important role whenever I was in the environment of a swimming pool, even though there were men everywhere in swimming trunks and every one of them happened to be gay. In this context only the sport counted for me. Now something else counted. I daresay I was the only one present in that swimming pool who did not regard himself as gay and did not think homosexuality a legitimate lifestyle, but it did not bother me.

Of course I met many friends and acquaintances. They soon noticed something had changed in my life and enquired what had happened. It was a special experience to be there as a new person in Christ, but when the contest was over, I had come to the conclusion that I had to close this book, however difficult it was to leave those friends and the life of swimming. In his grace, God helped me to do so. He sometimes breaks the leg of a lamb to protect it from itself. During one of the heats I injured my shoulder again. This time the injury was so bad that I not only had to pull out of the swimming competition but also had to give up the training for a while. In this way God weaned me away from the old life and nudged me on in a new direction.

I wanted to give expression to that new direction. In the Bible I read about baptism and in church I learned that this is a sign through which the believer expresses his choice of leaving the old life behind and starting a new life following Jesus Christ. As soon as I understood its meaning, it was the logical step to take. I had chosen to follow God and live a life in full obedience to him, so on the 15th February 1997 I was baptised. I wanted everyone I knew to witness my decision and had invited my parents. They came with fear and trepidation, wondering what kind of weird fanatic environment they were going to encounter. But they soon felt at ease when they noticed that the church consisted of ordinary people who were in fact very friendly and open. Over half of our congregation consists of people of Indonesian descent, who are known for their hospitality and for the delicious food they prepare. True to their tradition, they always prepare a lovely meal for any special occasion in church. So after the baptism service there was a meal for the whole congregation, and my parents were invited.

My parents' concept of 'church' was the stereotypical traditional picture of stiffness and solemnity. What they met here made them unwind. They appreciated the hospitality and friendship. They did not understand my conversion and the changes in my life, but at least they lost their fear that I had fallen into the clutches of a dangerous sect. Slowly they began to accept the new reality, just as they had accepted it when I broke the news that I was gay and had a friend. However, they kept quiet about it to the rest of the family and their friends. Whenever the news about my change got out, the reactions were negative. Many of those who had reacted positively when they first heard that I was gay were now upset that I did not want to go through life as gay any more. Some even rejected me.

At first my sister did not want to know of my change at

all. It seemed that my new-found faith and life had caused a permanent rift between us, which I greatly regretted as we had always been so close. Fortunately, as time went by, she came round and accepted the new reality. Our contact was restored, but it made clear to me that living for God in this world can have consequences in human relationships, not all of which are positive.

During the first few months of my life as a Christian, my friends would still frequently come by and often invited me to go out with them. Mostly I turned these invitations down. I did not fancy spending my time in pubs that reminded me of my past life. Sometimes I accepted an invitation and would accompany them to a pub, not with the aim of boozing, but in order to share the gospel with them. I would sit at the bar all evening and talk about Jesus Christ and what he had done for me. In fact it didn't matter where I was, whether a regular pub or a gay club; the only thing that interested me anywhere was to share my story. God's love was bubbling inside and needed a way out. I felt concerned for my friends. I had found real life and I knew that this was God's way for them as much as it was for me. I did not expect that it was within my power to turn them around, but I did want them to know that there was a better life. They must have got fed up with hearing my conversion story over and over again. In fact, soon I noticed they invited me less often. Obviously they did not feel completely at ease with me and my religious talk when in fact they had gone out with the purpose of having fun and drinking. And really I did not have any desire to go out any more. Slowly we grew apart and soon I lost contact with many of them, even my best pal Ronald.

The change in my life also affected my work. Everybody in the office had known me as the gay colleague. I had always openly owned up to my sexual identity and had often told about my escapades in the gay scene, sometimes with the aim of shocking some of the more proper colleagues. I had always liked to see how far I could go and had always enjoyed it when I registered some shocked reactions. Now, out of the blue, I came with my conversion story, and they did not know what to make of it. Some reacted with cynicism, others were wary – they would wait and see how long it lasted. Yet some of them could not deny that they saw a definite change in me. And it was a change for the better. I had not been happy in my job and they knew I had been suffering from depression.

What most of them didn't know was that I had made a mess of my work. It was a well-paid job and I had good colleagues, but I had lost all interest in my work. It had just become a means of financing my holidays, my sports activities and my life in the gay scene. My work had suffered because of this attitude, but I had been able to hide it from everybody. I had recently had a job evaluation with one of my superiors and had been able to mask the bad quality of my work. Now I felt guilty and unhappy about this, because I would have to keep up appearances and go on deceiving the people around me. I decided that following Jesus also meant that I should be honest and open about my work, so I requested another interview with my superior and told him what was bothering me: 'I recently had an evaluation and your impression was that I was performing well, but I want you to have another look at my work. In fact I have made a mess of it and I need help. I want to be honest about it. Sorry for hiding this from you for so long.'

He was speechless. With this information I had given him enough reason and justification to tell me to go and look for another job. I told him I had become a Christian and I was convinced that I should sort out not only my private life, but also my professional life. This rang a bell with him, as he had come from a Christian background. He didn't fire me, but gave me time to get my work sorted out, even offering his help. After that I produced better work and whenever I encountered any problems, I did not hesitate to inform him and ask for assistance. I did not mind what others thought of this. I was happy in my job again and did not have to keep up appearances.

In the meantime the counselling sessions at Different continued. After the first seven sessions with Johan, I moved on to group sessions in which the Living Waters material[2] was used. This really helped me, but also confronted me with things that still needed to be straightened out. In the course of my life many things had gone wrong in relationships, but also in my self-image and my communication with others. I had developed wrong patterns of behaviour. And in the course of these group sessions many of these issues came to the surface.

In one of those sessions, we were looking at what masculinity really is. The group leader asked us to write down the first ten things that came into our minds when reflecting on the concept of masculinity. The first thing that

---

[2] Living Waters is a course devised by Andy Comiskey, an ex-gay in the US leading a ministry similar to Different.

popped into my mind was a sight that is very typical to Holland: a father riding a bike through the busy traffic in Amsterdam, with a child in a child's carrier seat in front of him. To me, *that* was the ultimate symbol of masculinity. A splendid sight, although I never imagined that it could ever have its fulfilment in my life. It was an ideal. I never thought about a heterosexual relationship or children of my own. I just worked at the restoration of my own life and identity. But when dwelling on this picture of the father with his child on the bicycle, it influenced my thinking. Would it be possible to develop and grow towards that ideal?

This session became a turning point in my perception of masculinity. It helped me to develop a positive self-image. In our society, masculinity is associated with burliness, cars and motorcycles, soccer and other rough sports. Even in our group session these stereotypical elements were mentioned first. They did not suit me, but I became aware that it was wrong to limit masculinity to these elements. The symbol of the father with his child on a bike was much more real and masculine to me, whether it would ever be true in my own life or not. This image corrected my vision of my own masculinity and manhood in general.

I wanted to become the man God meant me to be. Often I felt unsure of how to act as a man. For many years I had lived nearly exclusively in the gay scene. That had been my world and my culture. My contacts with men had always had a certain suspense. Sexuality had played an important role in those relationships. Now I had to learn all over again how to relate to other men. I was out of tune with the heterosexual world. How does a heterosexual man behave?

Six months after my conversion I rarely had any contact with my old friends, and I entered a period marked by loneliness. My life had been so full of friends and social contacts, but in quitting the gay scene I had also lost most of my social life. That hurt, because it involved so many deep and warm friendships. Of course I had received much in return through my relationship with God. I also experienced a warm welcome and interest in the church, but the average age of the congregation was well above my years and this implied that there were very few of my peers. An ample social life had always been one of my basic needs. Now I was alone and beginning to feel sorry for myself. It was getting me down, and one day I urgently prayed about this problem: 'Please, Lord, what am I to do with this lonely feeling? I know you are there, but I feel I also need people with whom I can relate, folk who can help me in my spiritual life, friends with whom I can feel at home.'

The moment I said this prayer it was as though Jesus himself sat down beside me and put an arm around my shoulders. In a very special and intimate way I experienced his friendship. I knew he was there and I never had to be lonely any more. The sadness lifted and the loneliness evaporated. My relationship with God was strengthened and raised to a higher level. That gave me confidence that he would have a solution for any loneliness I would encounter in the future. With this same confidence I prayed: 'Lord, please teach me to make friends with other Christian men. Help me to make contact with them. I don't really know how to, but you are with me, and with your help I can do it. Please show me the way.'

From that moment onwards things began to happen.

Doors opened and I felt a boldness to make contact with other men. At first I sometimes still wrongly believed that I had to start talking about cars, as I felt uncertain what to talk about, sometimes fumbling for words. However, slowly but surely I began to get the hang of it and my contacts in the hetero world increased. And very soon the Lord was to lead me into new situations in which I would never lack friends, and loneliness would become a thing of the past.

12

Battle and Victory

It was a lovely sunny day in the early spring of 1998 and I decided to go for a stroll through town. The warm weather had lured many people outdoors and the centre of Amsterdam was alive with a pleasant hustle and bustle. As I enjoyed the glorious weather and observed the people around me, all of a sudden I felt strong homosexual desires flood my body and mind. This was the first time I had been confronted with such strong feelings since my conversion and it frightened me. What was going on?

Confused, I hurried home. I decided to spend some time in prayer. I felt restless and wanted to clean my thoughts up as quickly as possible. At the same time I felt upset with this new turn of events. Spiritual life had been exciting, but also hectic. So many changes had taken place and had claimed all my attention and energy. I had been confronted with so much that had gone wrong in my life and I had spent much time in cleaning up. I had changed the focus and orientation of my life, traded an old way of life for a new. And now, to top it all, I was confronted again with the old feelings.

All kinds of questions flooded my mind. What did this mean for my spiritual life? Was I back to square one? Did I have to start all over again? Was I messing things up? Did faith not work after all? The old feelings really frightened me. Would they be too strong for me, and drag me back to the life of compulsively seeking sexual satisfaction that I was so relieved to have left behind?

It was all too much for me and for a moment it felt as if I was losing control over my life – particularly my spiritual life. I couldn't keep up with God's pace. I was on my knees and begging God to give me a break. Things were going too fast for my liking. And I certainly had not counted on a further round of spiritual battle over strong sexual feelings. A short spiritual holiday seemed appropriate. I literally prayed: 'Lord, I want to continue with you, but please leave me in peace for a moment, without any further spiritual developments.' I thought I needed to change to a lower gear and take things a bit easier.

God answers our prayers, but often not in the way we would think best. That's what I found out 45 minutes later when the phone rang. It was Dina, one of the counsellors at Different.

'Richard, there is a missionary organisation in Amsterdam that has approached us with a request and I wondered whether you could help them. Every summer they organise evangelistic outreaches in the city, with teams of young people from all over the world. As the Gay Games are to be held in Amsterdam this year, these teams will meet many gays. They have asked us if we know someone with a gay background who would be willing to tell his story and help these teams to gain some insight into the gay scene. They need to be prepared to evangelise in that environment. Would you be willing to help out?'

To be honest, this was not the kind of answer to prayer that I had wanted or anticipated. But when at twelve o'clock you pray and ask God to give you a break from spiritual activities, and within an hour you are asked to tell the story of what he has done in your life in order to help others in evangelistic outreach, obviously God does not have a spiritual holiday in mind. He knew I needed something very different to help me on in my life with him. Previous experience had already taught me that his ways are always the best and that I could trust him unquestioningly.

After a moment's reflection, I said yes to Dina and immediately my uneasiness and feelings of depression were lifted. It felt as though I had changed to another train on my way to the next station in my life with God. This filled me with a thrilling sense of expectancy, as if God were saying: 'Do not be afraid. Just continue your walk with me. You may feel uncertain and think you don't have complete control over your life, but don't forget that I have everything under control.' Again I was filled with the reassuring conviction that whatever happened, God wasn't going to let me down.

At that time I did not do anything with the homosexual feelings that had manifested themselves again. I just ignored them. I had to do something with this reality, but I honestly did not know how to go about it. I think God helped me that day not to make these feelings my main focus and preoccupation. He would deal with them later. They shouldn't discourage me. Instead, God helped me to look forward.

I was invited to visit the mission organisation Youth With A Mission (YWAM) and meet Rebeca, a Mexican lady, who was in charge of the evangelistic outreach. Rebeca told me about the summer activities and her enthusiasm rubbed off on me. This was all new to me, but I was thrilled to be involved in helping others to communicate the gospel.

One month later, when all the summer teams were present, I went again to the YWAM centre to tell them about my life in the gay scene and how wonderfully God had saved and delivered me. Another speaker at the training sessions was Pat Lawrence from Canada. She is a counsellor and a member of Exodus International, a worldwide organisation of ex-gays. Pat gave excellent Bible studies on the subject of homosexuality.

I had once or twice been up in front of my church to tell the story of how God had saved me from my past life, but this was the first time I had talked about my life in front of an audience of total strangers. I felt very ill at ease and nervous. I did not think I was born to be a public speaker and it certainly is not easy to speak to 80 complete strangers about your deepest feelings. But as I got underway, I noticed that God gave me the words to express what was in my heart. Talking about the wonderful way in which he had revealed himself to me and changed my life, I was overwhelmed again by his love and could not hold back my emotions.

Several weeks later I had to address a second group of young people. This time the biblical teaching was given by Pat Caven from the US. Pat worked for Resurrection Life Ministries, an organisation that, like Different, provides counselling for sexually broken people. This was my first contact with a ministry that I would get to know really well a few years later.

At the end of the seminar, a young woman came up to me and introduced herself: 'I am Bianca and I work in Heidebeek, the training centre of Youth With A Mission up country. I want to invite you to come and tell your story at our centre too. Although only a limited number of the young people in Heidebeek will be in Amsterdam during the Gay Games, I think your testimony can help all of them.'

Suddenly I found myself involved in new activities. Instead of changing to a lower gear, it seemed the Lord was determined to speed things up. Afterwards I recognised God's wisdom in these events. Contact with young enthusiastic Christians and involvement in evangelism was exactly what I needed at that time. And telling my story so often, made me realise even more the absolute wonder of what God had done in my life. These activities were God's planning. It was his way of getting me out of the loneliness of my apartment. What I did not need at all was to sit at home alone, moping over my feelings, preoccupied with myself, and God knew that. He took me out of there and placed me in situations where I had to live out my new life in practice.

To meet people from organisations like Exodus International and other international ministries was a blessing to me. These were people who had gone through similar struggles to mine. I also greatly enjoyed the international character of Youth With A Mission. I felt at home at once and very soon I was asked to join them in some of the evangelistic activities during the Gay Games in August.

This was a completely new challenge to me. Suddenly it dawned on me that I was going to be there after all. Four years before, in New York, I had felt it my destiny to go back to Amsterdam as an 'evangelist' of the gay lifestyle and promote the Gay Games '98. Up to the moment of my conversion I had been heavily involved in the preparations. These experiences now seemed like something from a remote past that I could hardly remember. The Gay Games had completely faded from my horizon. Now, 21 months later, I was going to be there after all, but now with a totally different calling.

So one fine day in August I started out with a large group of Youth With A Mission folk, to attend the opening ceremony in the Arena, the large brand new soccer stadium on the edge of town. We did not go there with the purpose of evangelism, but just to be present, taste the atmosphere and pray for the work of the coming two weeks. As we walked to the Waterloo Square underground station to travel to the stadium, I saw that we were not the only ones! The train was packed with people going to the opening ceremony and we had a job to all squeeze on and find a place to stand. A 'pink' train it could be called, as it was packed with people from the gay scene. As I shuffled inside and tried to find a niche in which to stand, to my surprise I found myself looking into a familiar face. He was a member of the gay swimming club in The Hague.

'Hello, Richard, lovely to see you here. Long time no see. Are you taking part in the Games again?'

For a moment I was at a loss as to what to say and was

fumbling for words. 'Well, I will be there, but I'm not swimming.'

'What a pity! You will miss it.'

We got into an animated conversation and at one stage he asked me, 'What about your love life? Is there any special man in your life?'

'Well, I can say there is,' I replied, as I prayed in silence for wisdom.

'Do I know him?' he asked.

'I don't know whether you know him,' I said with some trepidation. 'It's Jesus Christ. I recently got to know him.'

My old friend was flabbergasted and it was written all over his face. This he hadn't expected, knowing the kind of wild life I used to live. He was dumfounded and this forced me to continue, right there in the middle of the compartment packed with gays. So I picked up the conversation and told him about my encounter with God. As I did, I forgot everything else around me. We were standing so close to others that undoubtedly many were forced to listen in on our conversation, but I did not notice. With great frankness I told him about God, about what Jesus Christ had done for me on the cross, how I had experienced his love and how much I loved him. My friend listened quietly, absolutely astonished at what he heard. I felt so thankful that I could share this precious message with someone from my old circle of friends. I testified how God had changed my life and forgiven my sins. There, right in the middle of a gay crowd going to the opening ceremony of the Gay Games, I also told him I did not live as a gay any more, because God had shown me that this was not his will and purpose for a man. It might not have been the most appropriate environment in which to talk about this subject, but it was so much part and parcel of what God had done in my life that it seemed natural to include this aspect. I experienced the fulfilment of the promise Jesus himself gave to his disciples when he said that they should not worry about what to say when asked to give account of their faith in him, because he would give them the words to speak.

Afterwards other members of the team told me how awesome my testimony had sounded among all the visitors of the Gay Games, many of whom evidently had followed our conversation with great interest.

The result of the encounter on the underground train was that all hesitancy on my part to speak about the gospel at the Gay Games had disappeared. During the opening ceremony I met other old acquaintances, including my old chum Ronald. He knew of course about my change and was very surprised to see me there. He wanted to know why I had come. In somewhat covert terms I told him about the purpose of our presence at the Games. In most conversations we could share a little about the gospel and we prayed that during the Games the Lord would give us open doors to share the message of his love.

These experiences helped me to take the next step. A few days later I travelled to the city of Amersfoort with a team of twelve young people, to evangelise at a location where the main swimming competitions of the Gay Games would be held. There I met many old friends, with some of whom I had taken part in international competitions just the year before. I had belonged to the core of the gay swimming scene and had always been present. When all of a sudden I did not appear any more, questions had been asked: 'Does he have a friend who doesn't approve of him travelling about so much?' 'Is he so badly injured that he had to stop swimming altogether?' 'Is he sick?' This last option was a serious and loaded question in the gay scene, as the terrible reality of AIDS was still very much a spectre in the background.

Some old friends knew exactly what had happened to me and had talked about it. Rumours that I had quit the gay scene had gone around, but at first they had been met with utter disbelief. Now many of them took the opportunity to ask me about it personally.

I had many good contacts during the swimming competition. There were about 1,100 participants and although not all of them were at the swimming stadium at the same time, there were always several hundred present. And I was amazed at how God led me to speak to those who were interested in talking to me. I was truly thankful that I could meet so many old friends who had meant so much to me and was able to share with them the message that now meant the world to me – the message every human being needed in order to find salvation and live a life as God intended. I told them that this was the reason I had come to the Games.

However, not only did I tell my story, but many old friends used the opportunity to tell me their story. Sadly some of the boys told me how they had grown up in a Christian home, but when they had broken the news that they were gay, they were given to understand that they were no longer welcome in the family. It was hard for me to comment on such stories. I had not realised that this could happen. It was so opposite to my experiences. My parents had never reacted with rejection or even reserve. Although I could very well understand that Christian parents would not be overjoyed at the news that their son or daughter was gay, I could not imagine that they would react with outright rejection. Surely that could not be God's way of dealing with this problem! Doesn't he have an answer even for this difficult situation?

My old acquaintances asked me many more questions, but I soon noticed that I often did not have the answers. My understanding of God's will and ways was still very limited.

The others on the team also made many good contacts during this sporting event. We had a deep desire to communicate God's love to these people. One gay sportsman from Mexico said in an interview with a secular newspaper that this was the first time he had met with Christians who did not condemn him.

Taking part in evangelism at the Gay Games had strengthened my faith and my determination to grow in my new life. In the first few months after my conversion, sexual feeling hadn't played any significant role in my life. My relationship with God had been so all-consuming that everything else had seemed to fade away. During that period I developed the erroneous and unrealistic notion that I would never feel any homosexual desires again. When they had returned, on that sunny spring day in Amsterdam, they had filled me with fear. I had been afraid that my old life would overwhelm me again; afraid that I would not be able to stand against the temptations; afraid that my Christian life would crumble and fall apart.

I had sidestepped the issue of these recurring sexual desires when I got involved with the evangelistic activities at the Gay Games, but I had not really dealt with it. I had thought that I would grow stronger by not paying attention to the temptations and at first I continued to deny the feelings, although deep in my heart I knew they were latently present. I thought I could overcome them by ignoring them. I took part in a support group at Different, where we discussed our experiences. Even there I still reacted in denial of my true feelings and continued to reaffirm my success story of the first months. This was in stark contrast to what others of the group shared. They told about their battles with sexual feelings and desire. My denial must have sounded strange to them, even arrogant.

My understanding of God's work in a person's life was still very limited. I thought God's work would suffer damage if I confessed to any weakness. I was afraid that owning up to weakness would convey the idea that God had not done his job very well. It seemed as if I wanted to protect my heavenly Father from failure. This would of course have been absolute arrogance, had I not been still very young in the faith and ignorant of many of God's ways.

Little by little I began to grasp that in spiritual life things work differently. Denying feelings doesn't solve anything. Johan had been right when he had told me that homosexual feeling could linger for quite a few years. I had to face the fact that this was the case with me. Temptations are a reality in the life of every human being, regardless of his or her sexual orientation. And so, one day in the support group, I had to confess that old feelings still played a part in my life. What I had to learn was to handle these feelings in the right manner.

The summer activities had given me a growing desire to be able to share the gospel with others. In my contact with non-believers I had noticed that my knowledge and experience were insufficient to communicate the gospel effectively. At the Youth With A Mission centre I had heard a lot about the Discipleship Training School (DTS) – a short-term course to prepare young people for evangelistic work. I very much wanted to do such a course, but I wondered whether I was ready for this. After all, I had been a Christian for only a year and nine months. Was it God's plan? I felt uncertain. It was already late in August and a new DTS course would commence in September. Should I enrol?

I wanted to take a break in order to settle this question, so I decided to take a holiday and go for a week to one of the Greek islands. Greece had always been my favourite holiday destination and I managed to book a last-minute flight to the island of Lesbos. It was the only destination with a seat available. There on Lesbos I found a very quiet spot under the trees in a secluded olive grove, where I could pray undisturbed. And during this time of prayer and Bible reading, God gave me the assurance that it was right for me to enrol in the DTS.

Yet this precious time with God did not mean I was free from the fight with temptation. During a visit to the beach of Lesbos my peace was rudely shattered when I met a man who tried to attract my attention, clearly with the aim of sexual contact. This situation immediately conjured up all kinds of memories. I felt the tension of the invitation, which even aroused me sexually. I knew I had to reject the invitation and I wanted to, but still it took some inner struggle before I was able to do so. I felt disheartened that victory still required such a battle. Why did I not make more progress? Why did it still take so much effort to resist? Why did those feelings come up at moments when I least expected them? Hadn't I just spent so many precious hours in prayer? Would I never be able to go to the beach any more because of the danger of meeting someone with amorous intentions towards me and arousing all the old reflexes? 'Lord, when is all this going to end? You know I don't want it!'

As I wrestled with God over these questions, he directed my attention to the letter of James in the New Testament. I did not understand why, but obediently I started to read. I had never yet read this part of the Bible, but as I began, the very first verses startled me: 'Consider it pure joy, my brothers, whenever you face trials of many kinds, because you know that the testing of your faith develops perseverance' (James 1:2–3). This was a completely different approach to temptations. Further on in the same chapter, the apostle writes: 'Blessed is the man who perseveres under trial, because when he has stood the test, he will receive the crown of life that God has promised to those who love him' (v.12).

Now things became clear to me. In this life we shall always be confronted with temptations, but God turns this negative fact into a positive thing by using this struggle with temptation to make us grow in faith and love for him. To live with God is not a decision that we take once only, but a decision we take every day or even many times a day. I am weak, but he gives grace and strength to say yes to him and no to every sinful and wrong desire that comes up. Each time this happens, I may choose again to follow him. Each time I make this choice, it brings me closer to him. God does not take away temptations. They are an integral part of this broken world of which I am a part. If he were to take away temptations, he would have to abolish my existence. God has a better way. He comes to me and I can draw strength from my relationship with him in order to resist the temptation. Every time this happens, my relationship with God is deepened and I am made stronger in my struggle against sin. This choice is a choice to love him.

This was not just theory. It became daily practice in my life. I did not look for temptations. On the contrary, the most stupid thing one can do is to abet these desires and play with wrong feelings. That is playing with fire. I knew I had to avoid dangerous situations. But when temptations did come, I used these moments not to fight the feelings, but to seek God and say yes to him. This turned many of these occasions into very precious moments with him.

Studying this first chapter of the book of James proved a major breakthrough in my life. From that moment on, I also knew that the hard battle against the homosexual feelings would not be a pattern that would mark the rest of my life, because the Lord would use these temptations to strengthen my faith and change my life. They would drive me closer to him. More than before I began to understand that my identity wasn't any longer in my sexuality, but in Jesus Christ.

Strengthened with these new insights and experiences I travelled to Heidebeek in September 1998 to step out in the next adventure with God. I was going to do the Discipleship Training School.

13

In the School of Christ

The initial DTS course of Youth With A Mission consists of two periods. The first 13 weeks are taken up with Bible study and subjects related to spiritual life, communication and evangelism. The second period of three months is a practical training on the spot in some mission situation. This course gave me the opportunity to spend some time concentrating completely on spiritual things and my personal relationship with Jesus Christ, together with a group of like-minded young people.

I shared a dormitory with six other young men. We spent much time together, discussing spiritual things, praying together and sharing the things that concerned us. In this environment I recognised that deep down there remained some homosexual inclinations from the past, but they hardly played any part in my daily life, even though I lived at close quarters with six others. Sexuality remained somewhat in the background. We were too busy taking in and understanding all the things God wanted to teach us. I noticed that the more I was fixed on my relationship with

God, the less I was perturbed by patterns and desires from the past.

The DTS course is intensive and hectic. After a busy day of lectures and studies I often withdrew for an hour to a quiet and beautiful spot on the heather, close to the YWAM base. Heidebeek is situated in one of the most splendid woodlands in Holland, broken by beautiful fields of heather. There in the stillness I would find rest in God's presence. I would tell him what was on my mind and often God spoke to my heart. That lonely spot on the heather became my meeting place with God.

One day as I sat there, praying and meditating on God's word, I looked up at the splendid cloud formations overhead. It had been a cloudy day, but gaps began to appear in the canopy and all of a sudden a magnificent bundle of rays penetrated the overcast sky – first in one place then, as the clouds broke, in other places. It was an impressive show of sunlight, and as the powerful rays transformed the scenery, it looked as though God was giving a visual display of how he reveals his love to us from heaven, as if he wanted to attract my attention in a very personal way. I was deeply impressed with the beauty of creation and the majesty of God. Again I tasted his love and grace. It became one of those moments of fellowship with God that words are inadequate to describe. It left an indelible impression on my heart and formed a milestone in my walk with God. I knew I belonged to him. I was fully accepted and I knew that my life was for ever bound to him.

During the course we regularly prayed for the practical mission period that would follow. We could choose between several destinations: Uganda, Brazil, Thailand or

Taiwan. Africa had always fascinated me and the Lord seemed to confirm this preference, so I put my name down for Uganda.

Shortly after finishing the course in Heidebeek we travelled to Africa, with a team of ten students and three staff members. Once in Uganda, we split up into smaller groups. Our group stayed at the YWAM centre, beautifully situated on the shore of the famous Lake Victoria.

The work of the mission station was led by a couple with two young children. I really felt at home there. The children often came to me to chat and romp. I greatly enjoyed having them around. Suddenly the thought struck me how wonderful it would have been if I could have been a father myself. Unfortunately, that did not belong to the realities in my life, and never would as far as I could see.

The evangelistic programme had been planned in detail beforehand. Back in Holland we had already done the necessary preparation, practising drama pieces, preparing evangelistic talks and testimonies. In the morning we would set out in an open jeep, driving along the dusty red dirt roads to far away villages in the bush, where our impending arrival had already been announced. Immediately upon entering the village we were surrounded by a multitude of excited and noisy children. The villages were poor and simple, a collection of very basic huts and houses. The largest building was generally the church. The hospitality of these poor people impressed us deeply. They had little to nothing, but they liberally shared the little they did have in a show of appreciation for our coming. I regard it as a privilege to have experienced their love and hospitality.

We greatly enjoyed our time with the village folk in

Uganda, but there was another side to our visit. Several of us contracted malaria, in spite of the prophylaxis we had taken, and we regularly suffered other illnesses. Yet much worse was the confrontation with the results of the HIV epidemic. We met many people who were bedridden and dying because of this disease. Part of our programme involved visiting sick people, hospitals, AIDS patients and children in orphanages. The various hospitals and institutions lacked everything, even the most basic elements such as doctors, beds and medicines. In the midst of this suffering you feel helpless and inadequate. We would have loved to be able to help people in these desperate circumstances.

Working in Uganda was a great experience and I had learned a lot during the DTS, but I had discovered that there was still a lot more to learn. Upon my return to Holland I enrolled in another more extensive course in Amsterdam, the School of Urban Missions. This 18-month course is also organised by YWAM and prepares people for urban mission work. The curriculum is divided up into periods of three months. Each block of three months of study is followed by three months of 'field training', with specific targets of putting into practice what one has learned in theory. Besides biblical studies, the course includes subjects such as comparative religion, cultural anthropology and pastoral counselling.

For my first practical period I was sent to Venezuela, with the assignment to learn Spanish and do a study of the culture. I was collected from the airport by someone who spoke only Spanish. That was quite a shock. She drove me to the house of a lady called Gloria, where I had a room for the duration of my stay in Caracas. Doña Gloria was the mother of Armando Benner, the leader of the YWAM base in Amsterdam and a very good friend of mine. She welcomed me in English, gave me a quick run down on the house and the surroundings and then said, 'Solo hablamos español' – 'from now on we will only speak Spanish'. In the weeks that followed I was to concentrate on learning the language, not through a language school, but by using a course in grammar I had brought with me and by communicating with the people, collecting and learning words.

I had a fixed programme. In the morning I first spent some time studying the grammar. Then I took the underground into town. This is an excellent means of transport to explore the city of Caracas. One of the goals was to make contact with people and try out the new sentences I had learned. This was quite a challenge.

One of the people I contacted was a half-paralysed boy who sat begging on a fixed spot on the Sabana Grande, the main shopping street in the city. Frequently I would stop and sit beside him to chat. Of course the conversation was very simple and I often repeated the same subjects, as my repertoire was very limited. We talked about the weather and the things going on around us, but I also tried to share the gospel. That wasn't easy with my very rudimentary command of the language and I don't know how much he understood. I noticed, however, that he really appreciated the attention and friendship.

During this period Armando Benner came to Caracas with his wife and children to visit his family. I enjoyed their company. Armando had been a great help to me in spiritual matters. During his visit to Caracas we often went out jogging together early in the morning. One day, as we were running again in Parque del Este, we sat down for a few moments in a shady spot to catch our breath and get away from the hot sun. We were chatting about our lives and at one stage in the conversation Armando asked me, 'What about love in your life?'

'What about love?' I repeated. 'Well, everything is fine. It's the Lord and me. That's sufficient for me. In matters of human love relationships and sexuality so much has gone wrong in my past that I have definitely closed *that* chapter of my life.' I meant what I said and had perfect peace with the idea. There were still the remains of homosexual feelings in my life, but I could handle these quite well and they played only a minor role. I had come to know that the love of Jesus Christ and meeting him was better than all else I had experienced. And another thing I knew for sure: I never wanted to return to my old lifestyle and I certainly did not think I needed a woman to confirm the change in me.

'Still, I believe that God created us in such a way that a man and a woman belong together,' Armando went on. 'I think it is very possible that God has a woman somewhere who is just the person to suit you and for whom you are the right man.'

I had not been prepared for this turn in the conversation and I tried to finish it: 'I am really grateful for the way in which God is at work in my life. But to start thinking about a relationship with a woman and about marriage is a bridge too far. I don't think I am ready yet for anything like that.'

Up to that moment I had never had any thought about a heterosexual relationship. I did not feel any inclination in that direction and could absolutely not imagine myself in that role. His questions did not strike a chord with me at all. It just did not seem to fit.

'But when will you be ready?' Armando insisted.

'I don't have the slightest idea,' I answered in all truth. I felt uncomfortable, but evidently Armando did not want to let it rest.

'Do you ever pray that God will send you the wife he has in mind for you?'

'No, that never crossed my mind.' It was something outside my reality. Why should I pray for something I did not feel the slightest need of?

Armando told me that he and his wife had started praying for the right partners for their children from the day they were born. He explained that this was one of the most crucial and important decisions in a person's life and therefore always a matter for much prayer.

'What do you think? Shall we pray that God will lead you to the right partner in your life too?'

Well, I couldn't possibly object to a prayer. I had absolute trust in God – that he knew what was best for my life – but I was quite convinced that he was of the same opinion as I was. To me it wasn't an urgent matter. On the contrary, I could not picture myself as a husband or father.

We prayed together that God would lead me according to his perfect will and that in his time I would meet the right woman. I was absolutely earnest in my prayer at that time, but even so I could not see how this prayer could possibly relate to my life. It wasn't a subject that occupied my mind and I prayed about it only two or three times after that day in Caracas, more in response to Armando's insistence than out of any personal desire. And when I did pray about it, there wasn't any urgency to see the prayer fulfilled. I left the matter with God.

Still, in some way this prayer together with Armando was another milestone in my life with the Lord, as it brought the possibility of a relationship again within my horizon, remote though it seemed.

The Christmas season was approaching as I arrived back in Holland a few months later. Before starting the second period of studies, I went for a short break to Heidebeek to attend a 'love feast', a special meal YWAM regularly organised for their workers for a time of fellowship and contact, meeting old friends again and establishing new friendships. At the end of one meal, I found myself chatting with Noêmia, a Brazilian woman working with the team in Amsterdam. I had seen her there on occasion, but had never had a chance to get to know her. We had an animated conversation and as the evening wore on it seemed as though we had known each other for years. Our colleagues and friends went to bed one after the other until only the two of us remained. We continued to talk into the small hours. We shared a passion to make the love of Jesus Christ known to the people of the inner city of Amsterdam. Although we came from very different backgrounds we seemed to have a lot in common. This meeting made a deep impression on me. I cannot say that I felt I was falling in love, but this woman struck me as very special. I felt strongly attracted to her, not physically, but spiritually. The next day, when writing an account of the previous evening in my diary, I jotted down the question: 'Lord, is she the one?'

I asked myself this question very reluctantly. Did I dare to think in that direction? Was it not much better to avoid such ideas? Wasn't I fooling myself if I allowed the thought that a relationship with a woman was possible? Suddenly Armando's prayer became a serious matter.

I had to leave it there, because shortly afterwards Noêmia left for Brazil for a period of four months. She was going to visit her family and the churches that supported her. Some time after she had left I overheard one of her colleagues comment: 'I wouldn't be surprised if Noêmia came back married.' To my own astonishment I felt a strong disappointment hearing this remark. *What a pity*, was my reaction. *But why am I disappointed?* I questioned myself. The answer was that meeting Noêmia had meant more to me than I had realised at the time. I had to admit that I could not easily forget our long and serious conversation. My interest in her went further than just a friendly contact. However, this admission came at a time when there seemed little hope of a follow-up on the contact. I reckoned that if her friends expected her to return from Brazil married, then she probably had plans in that direction and most likely had a friend or fiancé back home. I had to surrender this matter to God, yet I couldn't get her out of my mind.

After the second term of studies I spent a three-month practical period working with Mercy Ministries in The Cleft, the YWAM centre in the red light district of Amsterdam. I felt drawn to this kind of work because I had a passion for Amsterdam and I saw so much need in that part of the city, so many broken people, so much sexual brokenness. I knew from experience how this could mar a person's life. I felt a strong desire to share the love of Christ in that dark part of the city.

Up until then I had not had any inclination to evangelise specifically in the gay scene. I was just glad that I had been able to close that chapter of my life and leave it all behind. But while working in the inner city I had a growing wish to reach out to my old environment. As I thought and prayed about this, I was convinced that I needed more experience in counselling gays. As I discussed this with the lecturers of the Urban Mission School, it was suggested that I should spend my last practical outreach phase working with Resurrection Life Ministries in the USA. This ministry runs a pastoral counselling programme using the Living Waters course, which helps people with sexual and relational issues. The course takes people through an eight-month programme of study and counselling. During this time participants meet once a week. Participating in this work would be a unique opportunity to get to know the Living Waters material in depth and gain experience in counselling people who seek a way out of the homosexual lifestyle. My own experience would be a great help. The normal practical period of the Urban Mission School only lasted three months, but understandably Resurrection Life Ministries required that if I were to help in the counselling, I had to commit myself to the full eight-month programme. I gladly did so.

However, a few months before leaving for Atlanta something happened that would impact my life radically. Noêmia returned from Brazil still unmarried. More importantly, there wasn't the slightest indication that she had had any plans in that direction. My interest in her had not faded, but rather grown, and soon after her arrival I noticed that the interest was mutual. As if it were the natural thing to do, we began to seek each other's company, and during the summer of 2000 our friendship gradually became more intimate.

This was entirely new to me. For so long I had lived in a world in which women had played such a different role. And to be honest, after my conversion my approach to women hadn't really changed. Now it did change and this also meant some internal tension and uncertainty. *Imagine we got married. . . how would that be? What would it mean?* My past relationships had been marked by a great measure of freedom and open-endedness. When after some months or a few years it did not satisfy any more, or became too dull, you just broke up. Marriage was a different kettle of fish. It entailed a real and life-long commitment.

And of course there was the sexual aspect of marriage. Could I handle this? To be honest, it scared me. In the early stages of our courtship I avoided any thought of the sexual dimension of our relationship. Just continuing as very close and intimate friends, sharing a life together, seemed the ideal to me. Yet I knew that this was not a realistic way of looking at a relationship with a woman. To be sure, at first it was particularly the warm friendship and her character that attracted me to Noêmia, but as our relationship progressed and deepened, slowly the sexual attraction developed and I was able to overcome my anxious doubts in this area.

On the 9th September we announced our courtship officially to our friends and colleagues in Youth With A Mission. A week later I flew to Atlanta to work with the Living Waters programme, so the first few months of our courtship consisted of telephone calls and letter-writing. In the latter

I must confess that Noêmia was much more faithful than I was. The many new contacts and new activities in Atlanta claimed most of my attention and time.

All those working on the Living Waters programme as co-ordinators or small group leaders first have to attend a week of leadership training and preparation. Not only did we receive instructions on how to handle the course material and lead the groups, but during this week we also had to look at our own lives and see what might have gone wrong in the past, for instance in relation to our parents or in friendships. These aren't always dramatic or disruptive problems. They can be small and sometimes seemingly insignificant, but still they can have long-lasting effects on the emotional development of a child.

During one of the sessions in which we were assessing our own development, we had to answer questions about our relationship with our father. Had there been anything in our experience with our father that had disappointed or hurt us? Or was there anything in which we felt we had not been able to live up to his expectations? These questions were familiar, as I had gone through similar sessions when taking part in the support groups of Different. *I have already cleared all those matters,* I thought to myself, when looking at the questions.

At the end there was an opportunity to come for special prayer if the answers to the questions had brought up anything that bothered us. Perhaps God wanted to reveal something about the past experiences. I did not think that there was anything left to be discovered about the relationship between me and my parents that was still bothering me, but I decided to go for prayer anyway. The person praying with me stopped suddenly and said, 'The Lord seems to be pointing me to something that had an impact on your relationship with your father when you were a child and which is still a problem. It has to do with flowers.'

As he said this, the memory of my dad taking me out to the seaside to kick a football about came forcefully into my mind. He couldn't really get my attention on the ball because I was only interested in picking flowers. My parents had so often told this anecdote when we had visitors that I had unconsciously concluded that I had not lived up to certain expectations. As this all came back to me, something snapped inside. It was a very emotional moment. I brought this event and all the consequences to God. It seemed such an insignificant little detail, but it had marred my life more deeply than I had realised. It was just one wrong stitch, but it had had far-reaching results in the pattern that evolved. This was a very special moment in my life. God not only revealed the wrong stitch, but in his love and grace he took it up and corrected it. This was one more step that helped me to regard myself as God had meant me to be.

In hindsight it is so easy to see God's hand in all these events. The Living Waters programme was a very important preparation for what was ahead of me. I needed this to be able to build up my relationship with Noêmia, who was waiting for me back in Holland. So many big and little things had gone wrong in the past that could hinder a healthy development of a stable relationship, but God continued his work of restoration and healing. And of course he did so not only in my life, but in Noêmia's life as well. The Lord had his special way in her life; a life that had begun very differently, in the 'favelas', the slums of Brazil. It had been a difficult life, but one that was marked by the grace and love of God just as much as mine.

Incredibly Noêmia had first heard me share my testimony during the Gay Games back in 1998. She had been deeply impressed and felt attracted to me, but we did not have the chance back then to get to know each other. Noêmia had been abused as a child and, having had many bad experiences with men, told herself she would never start a relationship – yet she longed for companionship and prayed that God would lead her to someone with whom she could serve him.

Looking back, it is clear that God had plans for us both and had drawn our lives together.

14

Everything New

In December 2000 I briefly interrupted my work for the Living Waters programme in order to finish my studies at the Urban Mission School in Amsterdam and to graduate with my bachelor's degree in urban missions. Above all I was looking forward to being with Noêmia again. Courtship at a distance is not ideal for building up a relationship and we were glad to be able to spend some time together again. It wouldn't be long though, as I had committed myself to the full eight months of the Living Waters programme. I had to return to the USA in January for the remaining five months.

While in Holland I needed to arrange a visa, which is necessary when planning to stay in the USA for a period longer than three months. Working with Resurrection Life Ministries I needed a 'visa for religious purposes'. I thought that getting this visa would be a mere formality, but one week before returning, a missionary told me that she knew of cases in which people had had to wait for more than a year to get theirs. This worried me, as it would really spoil my plans. I could of course apply for a tourist visa, but that would be dishonest. I wanted to be open about my activities and felt that as God had called me to this job, he would also supply the visa.

So, armed with an official invitation from Resurrection Life Ministries and other documents, I went to the American consulate as quickly as possible. The man at the other side of the counter took my papers, glanced at them and shoved them back: 'This is not sufficient. You'll have to give more information for your application to be considered.'

That was an unexpected turn of events and I left rather dejected. At home I spent some time in prayer: 'Heavenly Father, I want to walk the royal way and do not want to use a ruse and travel on a tourist visa. I know that you are able to get me the right visa in time.'

I sent an email to Mike and Pat Caven in Atlanta to explain the situation and to ask for more formal information. They sent me only a little in addition to what I already had. It did not seem much and hardly sufficient for another serious attempt, but I decided to put in the application anyway. That same day the Lord encouraged me through the Bible story that tells how the Israelites, on their way from Egypt to the Promised Land, asked permission to go through the territory of Edom. The Edomites refused, and the Lord led them around that country, so in the end they did arrive at their destination. God could do the same for me.

The next day I went to the consulate again with the same papers and the meagre addition to the information. To my relief there was a different man behind the counter. He looked at my application, took my passport, stamped it and started to fill in the details and dates. 'Five months is not very long,' he remarked. 'Don't you think it would be better if I gave you a visa for ten years?'

I couldn't believe my ears. After the flat refusal the day before, I had not expected such obliging treatment. *Accept it and get out of here before he changes his mind*, I thought to myself as I thanked him profusely. God's ways are perfect and his detour turned out to be the best route. I quickly went to the travel agent's to get a ticket and managed to get a very cheap fare. Again I saw how God went before me.

In January I was back in Atlanta for the next five months of the Living Waters course. This meant a long period of separation from Noêmia, so we had arranged that she would come for a two-week visit some time in March. I was determined to make it a very special time. By now I was absolutely sure of my love for her and I wanted to propose to her during the visit. We were both convinced that the Lord had led us to each other and I was ready for the next step. I asked Mike Caven for his advice and he helped me to pick out a ring. I looked forward with anticipation to the day I could present it to Noêmia.

During her visit I took her out to a very special Italian restaurant. I had arranged the dinner beforehand and had given the ring to the chef, with the request that he incorporate it into the dessert. He turned it into a work of art! When the dessert was served, Noêmia saw the ring and I asked her to marry me. It was like a dream. Before we met I had already reconciled myself to the thought that I would remain single. Likewise Noêmia, though she had always had a small hope that maybe some day she would meet a

man to share her life and ministry with, she had accepted
the fact that most likely she would have to continue alone.
Both of us had known brokenness in the area of relationships and sexuality, but we had both been delivered and
healed by God. To both of us his love was the most important factor in life and it would have been sufficient for us. Yet
God gave us so much more than we ever could pray for or
imagine.

The weeks passed very quickly and Noêmia had to return
to Holland before we knew it. In the meantime we had
already discussed a wedding date and suggested that, if possible, we would like to get married that same year.

Apart from Noêmia's visit, the long months in Atlanta
were often marked by loneliness. The major activities of
the Living Waters course only took one day a week. The
rest were spent in preparation, study and prayer. During
these days I often felt lonely, and in such moments I
sometimes had the hardest battle to fight with recurring
sexual desire. This desire wasn't directed at another person. It wasn't temptation through falling in love with anyone, nor a longing for a sexual partner. These desires were
bare cravings for sexual gratification, as I had known during the years I had been addicted to sexual experiences. I
had learned how to handle such situations by saying yes
to God and no to the temptation. Yet these temptations
were not always overcome without a battle, and at times
I was discouraged that they kept recurring. Was this struggle to last for life?

One day I prayed, 'Lord, you give me the victory each
time, and I do not give in to that which my body craves
for. But I would like to go further. I do not only want to

get victory, but I want to celebrate the victory with you, like Israel in the Bible celebrated the victories you gave them.'

And God answered this prayer. From then on temptation wasn't only an opportunity to reject that which was wrong, but it became an occasion to feast with God. I experienced his love and confirmation in a special way. I knew that it was only through his power that I could resist sin, but still in this deep joyful fellowship with God I experienced, as it were, a festive reward; a party for two. God wasn't far removed from me during moments of temptation, as if it were something he did not want to have anything to do with. On the contrary, especially in these moments he was close to me, helped me through and rejoiced with me in the victory. This experience greatly enlarged my view of God's greatness and goodness.

There were a few more important decisions ahead and I used my time in Atlanta to pray about these. I had completed my studies, we were planning our wedding and now I needed to know God's plans as to our future work. By now I had a growing desire to evangelise in the gay scene and help people who wrestle with sexual brokenness. I saw this as a task God might have for me in the future, but I did not know how to go about it. The staff at Different had suggested at one time that they would like to see me join their ministry. On the other hand, there might be the possibility of doing a similar work within YWAM. Or did God want us to start something new on our own?

One sunny day I was pondering these matters and reading my Bible. I was studying the fourteenth chapter of the book of Mark and had reached the part where Jesus sends out two disciples to prepare the feast of Passover. They don't know where to go, but Jesus tells them they will see a man carrying a jar of water. They are to follow him and he will lead them to an upper room, where everything will be ready for them. They obey this unusual command, fully trusting in Jesus Christ.

Reading this, I understood that this was also God's answer to my questions. I did not have to be anxious about the future. We only had to follow on, step by step, trusting God to lead us in the right direction. He had a place fully prepared for us, and at his time he would show us what to do. We only had to be faithful in that which he had shown us already. This knowledge gave me peace. It also helped me to see that the first step would be to continue in the work of The Cleft, in the red light district of Amsterdam, where I had been active and where Noêmia was already committed. How my ministry would develop, God would show me in his time.

The first important matter to be looked into when arriving back in Holland was the arrangements for our wedding. At first we had picked the 10th September 2001, counting on the mild late summer weather to co-operate. For various reasons the date had to be postponed to the 2nd November, a bleak time of the year as far as weather is concerned, usually guaranteeing cloud, wind and rain. However, in spite of these expectations, the day turned out to be sunny and exceptionally warm for the time of the year.

My friends Mike and Pat Caven had come from the USA to attend our wedding and they accompanied me as I went to collect Noêmia in the morning. She had stayed with some friends who had an apartment on the second floor of a typical old Amsterdam tenement building, and this was where she got ready and put on her wedding dress.

We rang the doorbell and as the door opened, I saw her coming down the steps in a beautiful white dress, quite traditional with a veil and a train. She looked so beautiful! I was absolutely speechless. Pat Caven remarked to me afterwards, 'You should have seen your face when Noêmia came down the stairs. Your mouth just dropped open. You were radiant.' The old apartment block lacked anything remotely romantic, but Noêmia fully made up for it.

As is customary and required by law in Holland, we went to the local magistrate first, to register our wedding in a civil ceremony, which was attended by my family and a few close friends. In the afternoon we went to church for the main wedding ceremony, the highlight of the day. All our friends and colleagues from YWAM were there, as well as many members of my church, my family and the friends at Different. It was a very special service, in which the pastor and Armando Benner shared the official part. Together they prayed for a special blessing on our marriage. It was an unforgettable moment.

In the evening a feast was laid on for all our guests. Amsterdam is a very international city, with churches of many nationalities, and we had asked the Brazilian church to provide the music at the party. It was Christian music, but typically South American; the sort of music that automatically causes your feet to dance. It was a terrific and joyful party, but above all an expression of gratefulness for what God had done in our lives.

After the wedding we had a few days to sort out our things and pack our suitcases before we flew to Brazil. We had decided to spend our honeymoon in Noêmia's home country in order to be able to visit her loved ones and for me to be introduced to them. But before meeting her family and friends we spent ten days together at the beach, just the two of us. We wanted to be able to enjoy each other's company and get used to one another. There was still so much to be learned and discovered about each other. We had a lovely room in a good hotel in Caraquatatuba in the state of São Paulo, and we enjoyed the beautiful beach and the ocean, but above all we treasured each other's company.

After ten unforgettable days we travelled to Jacareí to meet some of Noêmia's family. By now I knew many by name and had spoken to some on the phone, but had never seen any of them.

For Noêmia it was a very emotional moment to arrive in her old surroundings as a married woman. They had prepared a warm welcome for us. I am rather communicative by nature and I found the language barrier somewhat frustrating, wanting to say so much and to hear even more, but always having to turn to someone to interpret for me. Still, we had a wonderful time with her family. Noêmia enjoyed being in her home town again with her relations and friends.

There was only one drawback in our visit to Brazil. Whenever we walked outdoors together, people often looked at us with evident disapproval or even hostility. With my blue eyes and Dutch appearance I was easily identified as a foreigner. The prejudiced locals quickly concluded that I must be a rich foreigner, a Gringo – an American – most likely, who had come over and paid a lot of money to a Brazilian girl to have a few weeks of fun before dumping her again and returning home. To Noêmia this attitude on the part of the townspeople was really hurtful, especially because of her past. It bothered her so much that at times she'd rather stay inside than go out with me. We talked about it together and I tried to comfort her: 'They don't know what they are looking at, Noêmia. Their prejudice is their problem, even though it hurts us. Every time someone stares at us, we must remind ourselves of the miracles God has done in our lives. Nobody can take that away from us. Other people's bad thoughts do not change this reality. In fact they only accentuate the grace of God in our lives.'

Both our lives feature the great change that God can work in a person. That doesn't mean we never experience struggles against sin or moments of weakness. Even now, old feelings can still linger in the background. They are not very strong and they are by no means continuous, but they are undeniably recognisable at times. I have to admit that they exist, but I also have to identify them for what they are: remnants of an old lifestyle. These are feelings that make me say yes to God and no to acts that are not in accordance with God's will and purpose.

These remnant feelings do not in any way hinder a happy relationship with my wife. I don't think my plight is very different from anyone else's. Any other married Christian man might feel excited by the flirtations of another woman. There may even be personal circumstances to make a response very tempting. Yet through

God's grace the husband recognises this danger, says yes to God and his wife in his heart, and turns away from the temptation.

Returning from a lovely holiday in Brazil, we picked up our activities in Amsterdam again. I had shared my vision for the gay scene with the leaders of YWAM, and although they agreed there was a need, they did not feel the time was right and advised me to start in the existing ministry. In hindsight I can see how wise this was. So many changes had taken place in my life in such a short time that starting new things and intensifying my contacts with the gay scene might not have been helpful to our marriage at this early stage.

Six months after our return to the work, the couple who were leading the work in The Cleft informed the team that they had accepted an invitation to another task in South Africa. We were asked to take over from them. This was undoubtedly a great challenge. We prayed about the request and believed the Lord was leading us to accept. Yet there were a number of friends who counselled us not to take on such a heavy responsibility in the first year of our marriage. Just as an Israelite in Old Testament times was exempt from army service during the first year of his marriage, they thought that we should apply the same principle and take time to work on our relationship. We listened to this advice and agreed to take over after our first wedding anniversary.

This proved to be wise counsel, especially in view of another big change that very soon announced itself. In February 2002 we discovered that Noêmia was expecting a baby. We had certainly hoped for this to happen, but it happened sooner than we had expected. We had both already turned 40 and had wondered whether it was still going to be possible. We were very happy. From the beginning we both had the idea that it was going to be a boy and we wanted to call him Pedro. Strangely enough we never thought about picking a girl's name. A little girl would certainly have been most welcome, but to be honest, I longed for a son.

In spite of the joy, it wasn't an easy time for Noêmia. As her pregnancy progressed, she suffered increasing ill-health. And when the nine months were over, nothing happened. When after two weeks the pains started, the doctor thought it wise to put her in hospital. There were problems with the delivery and after a very difficult night the doctors decided to do a caesarean. Those were very difficult moments, but when the doctor held the baby up and said, 'It's a boy!' all tension left in a wave of emotion and relief. Although this moment was the beginning of something completely new, I had the feeling it was also a grand finale. It seemed the crown on a long period of struggle, healing, restoration and new beginnings. It was such a great experience, so unbelievably beautiful!

Everything was fine with the baby, but very soon it was clear that things weren't at all well with Noêmia. Soon after arriving home she had to be rushed to hospital again, where she spent six very difficult weeks. At one stage the doctors even feared for her life. A lot of prayer went up for Noêmia in Holland, as well as in Brazil, and we are so thankful to our heavenly Father for restoring her to full health again.

Becoming a father was a major milestone in my life. It

changed my thinking and my conduct. All of a sudden I became aware that I was a father, a man with the responsibility for a son. Then the image came back to me of the man on the bicycle with his child in a seat in front of him. Incredibly that vision was coming true. Of course I would have to wait a bit before I could take Pedro out on a bike, but it wasn't far off any more.

Pedro Nathaniel David is the name we have given him. He is named Pedro after my father's name Peter, but to include his Brazilian background we have used the Portuguese form of the name. To my parents it was an unexpected blessing and joy to become Granny and Grandad. This was their first grandchild! Nathaniel means 'gift of God'. We added this name because that is how we regard him, and the name David because of our desire that he may worship God, our heavenly Father, who has been so unbelievably gracious to us, through his Son Jesus Christ our Saviour. He has shown us so much love and has done such great miracles in our lives. We can only bow down in worship and thankfulness before him, lift our hands up to him and confess that we can never find the words that will adequately express the thanks and praise we owe him.

This is our testimony of salvation, deliverance and healing, which God offers all of us in his Son Jesus Christ. This is the precious message of hope that we so long to share with all our loved ones – our families, our friends, our neighbours in the red light district and also all my old friends in the gay scene. We dedicate this book to you all and especially to my parents, who kept loving me as their son in all circumstances.